SWINFORD FAMILY PORTRAIT IN SHORT STORIES

Don Swinford

authorHOUSE®

AuthorHouse™
1663 Liberty Drive
Bloomington, IN 47403
www.authorhouse.com
Phone: 1 (800) 839-8640

Published by AuthorHouse 03/31/2016

ISBN: 978-1-5246-0072-3 (sc)
ISBN: 978-1-5246-0073-0 (hc)
ISBN: 978-1-5246-0071-6 (e)

These are true stories with only a couple of exceptions that are clearly evident. Stories from the recesses of my mind and other stories shared with me by family members. By in large, these are very personal stories that mean more to me than anyone else, but I'm sharing them because they may contain insight into my parents, my siblings, or me that others will enjoy knowing.

I am the youngest son of Ruby and Adren Swinford, and these stories cover a century of life, laughter, trials, and tears. Following are accounts of my youth, my parents, my siblings and other family members. I write of my military experiences, my work experiences, and the few years I spent in politics. Expressing my memories would not be complete without writing about my pets. We all have a story, but not all of us have the desire or time to write them down. Just think of the treasure we would have if our parents and grandparents had left us something in writing, telling us the lives they lived before our time. This didn't happen in my family, so I hope my children and grandchildren will put some value in my efforts to tell them these stories in writing.

I also hope this brings back some fond memories for each of you in the family. If it can bring a chuckle or a tear to your eye, I will consider my book a success. I was inspired to do this by reading short stories other friends had written. Important to me is the fact that I still have the memories when most all my siblings are gone or cannot do what I can still do. I've been blessed. I hope some of you are inspired to do the same. You know things that generations to come deserve to know. Why don't you sit down and write them and send me a copy. Most of all I want to thank God for the parents who gave me life and the chance to be part of what I believe is a wonderful family, and a wonderful legacy.

CONTENTS

THE COURAGE IT TOOK

History indicates that it took the Mayflower 65 days to travel 2500 miles to the new world. Granted, the Mayflower was not a good sailing boat. Even so, how long do you think it took another ship one hundred and forty years later to go from the last port of call in England to Baltimore, a total of 3500 miles? At best it was probably at least 35 days.

To the best of our knowledge, this is the trip that James and Elizabeth Swinford took with two young sons sometime around 1765 to reach America. Can you imagine the conditions on a ship like that for 35 days? With two sons less than ten years old, this took a lot of courage. It wasn't just our ancestors; it was hundreds of thousands of immigrants before ship travel was modernized.

That was just the first step. How did they survive once they got here? They had to have funds of some kind to sustain them while they found a way to make a living. There was no employment office and not that much of a civilization. It's not known how long they stayed in the Baltimore area, but eventually they ended up in North Carolina where James farmed. His two sons Elisha and Joshua married sisters there, Thankful and Mercy Doan, and from the Kentucky 1792 census it shows that James moved with his sons and families to that location in Harrison County. No mention of his wife Elizabeth who may have died before the move. There was also at least one son, John, who is believed to have been born after they arrived from England. He would have been in his late teens by the time they got to Kentucky.

Elisha and Joshua both had large families, as did John. Some of the male members of Elisha's family moved on into Indiana, then Illinois and Missouri. Joshua had more daughters than sons and had two marriages, and they more or less settled in Kentucky. All of John's sons were born in Kentucky and to our knowledge, only Elisha Simpson moved on to Indiana and then Illinois where he died in about 1856 in Coles County, Illinois. He had married Mary Grogan in Green Castle, Indiana, Putnam County, in the twenties and they had one daughter and six sons. The six sons settled in Illinois and the daughter married and stayed in Indiana.

With the exception of William Culwel, the sons of Elisha Simpson settled initially in Coles County. William went north to Champaign County. Three of the sons were in the Army with George and John Theodore seeing action. Elisha Newton entered after the end of the Civil War but did not leave Illinois. The youngest son Matthew Simpson was born in 1849 just before the move to Illinois. His mother Mary had the task of raising the younger children on her own after her husband died. She lived into the 1890's. Her daughter who married and stayed in Indiana had two sons, and each of her sons had sizeable families with the exception of George who was injured in the Army. He instead raised a niece of his wife and adopted a son named Frank Whiteside. He had eleven children with the name of Swinford.

All of the children were farmers and all had land, some more than others. My grandfather Matthew had eleven children with Rachael Elizabeth Digby and lived most of their married lives on the bank of the Embarrass River in Coles County on eighty acres. Rachael was his sister in laws niece that she and George had raised. Her name was also Rachael Digby before her marriage to George. Matthew and Rachael's youngest was a son named Albert Adren Swinford, born in 1903 and died in 1983. You know the rest of the story.

DOMINANT NAMES OF THE U.S.A

Many people have grown up with the same assumptions that I have due to the fact that teachers and others have used certain names in illustrating or teaching us. The names Brown, or Smith, or Jones rolled easily off their tongues and consequently that must be the most common names. Well, most people have not been to Coles County, Illinois. That is the county in central Illinois where Abraham Lincoln's father settled with his wife Sara Bush Lincoln. They lived just south of the county seat of Charleston and near the Kickapoo State Park that my brother helped build, but that was a hundred years later.

My brother was only sixteen when he joined F.D.R's Conservation Corp in the depth of the depression. He convinced my dad that he wanted to go, although under aged. It was less than twenty miles from home but the Corp provided living quarters and he only got to come home on weekends. My brother Dale tells the story of looking out across the fields in the cold winter and seeing Owen walking home, wearing a long coat, the type worn by the soldiers in the First World War. He was ready to get out, but my dad told him he had to finish the job.

The Swinford's migrated to Coles County in the mid and late 1840's. They put down stakes just four miles from Charleston and starting farming the land. This consisted of two clans of the Swinfords with a considerable number of males. By the turn of 1900 they had many acres of land in Coles County and the name had become very prevalent. The Lincoln name was gone and the Jones and Smiths were few and far between, but everyone knew a Swinford. Not only that, but many more had migrated from Kentucky to Indiana and Missouri and coupled with some distant relatives that arrived in South Carolina in the 1670's, the name has grown like wildfire.

A Civil War census indicates that as many Swinfords fought for the South as the North. Three of my great uncles were in the Union Army. In the last sixty years many of the middle states Swinfords have settled in the western states of California, Arizona, and Texas. I haven't been in a classroom for years but I wouldn't be surprise if the illustrators are now using our name instead of Jones, or Adams, or Obama.

ONE HUNDRED YEARS

In the year 2017 the Swinford family will celebrate its one hundredth annual family reunion. What started on a small farm in Coles County, Illinois in 1918 has stayed the course through wars and depressions to bring this proud family the fourth Sunday in August of each year to share one another's lives.

The first reunion was hosted by Frank and Nell Swinford and was well attended by the children and grandchildren of the family patriarchs that came to Illinois in the mid and late 1840's. Frank himself was an adopted son of George and Rachael Swinford, George being born in Putnam County, Indiana. I knew the white haired old gentlemen back in the 1940's as he attended the same church as I did with my folks and he was quite the gentlemen. I didn't know or understand until years later that he was adopted and was the father of eleven children. Our pastor was his daughter-in-law. To me she was Sister Florence Swinford.

A few years later the reunion moved to the park by the lake in Oakland, and in the thirties it moved to Paris, Illinois where the facilities were larger and had more entertainment for the youth. The numbers in attendance has varied over the years with the forties being the highest when some years the number almost reached three hundred. Only in the later years has the number fallen below one hundred.

All the children, grandchildren, and most of the great grandchildren of the Patriarchs have died off, and while there is some representation of some of them, most of the attenders are the descendants of Adren and Ruby Swinford, my father and mother. They had eight children and thirty-two grandchildren who have done much to carry on the tradition and not only will make it a Century event but move on into the second Century, holding the Swinford banner high.

ALOHA FROM HAWAII

I've never been to Hawaii, but I have had greetings from there. It all started in World War II when my brother Owen was drafted into the army. He had aspirations for the Army Air Corp but Uncle Sam had other ideas. He was sent to special schools to learn to maintain large generators. As it ended up, he was not in the Air Corp but spent two years in the South Pacific supporting air fields with power. Plane takeoffs and landings in the dark required lit run ways and his job was to see that they had power. He tells of hearing flights leave at night making their bombing runs and then returning before dawn and he would try and count the numbers.

On his way to the Far East in early 1944, Owen had a short stopover in Hawaii and that is when he sent each of his siblings a greeting. Wow, the best greeting I ever had at that age. It was a Hawaiian Dollar Bill. Hawaii wasn't yet a state, so the Hawaiian Dollar was a U.S. Dollar with Hawaii stamped on it. It spent like any other U.S. Dollar and I truthfully can't remember how fast or for what I spent mine, although I have a pretty good idea. It apparently did not last long enough.

Sister Edna received her dollar and was a little more frugal. So frugal that most of it was still sitting on her chest in her room when her little brother noticed it after his was all gone. Apparently he had gotten accustomed to the high life style and couldn't resist borrowing her change. At age 7 he fully expected to repay it.

The day's events began two blocks down the street on the other side of the square at a gas station where candy and sodas were available. With her change in his pocket, sis's little brother didn't want to stay too close to home as he might be seen eating and drinking too much by one of his several siblings. Later, movies were only nine cents so that seemed the place to go for the afternoon. The popcorn and candy was reasonable there. It was an intense war picture about the Germans taking over small villages and the battles they were having with the men and women of those villages. He learned how the villagers would stretch wire between trees across roads to decapitate the motorcyclist and how terrible war was. The movie made a lasting impact on him.

When the feature ended, it was not the practice to empty out the theatre and start over as long as there was no seat shortage, so he still had more change for another round of popcorn, candy, and drinks and he just stayed on. Supper time came and went and although the money was now gone, he was super tired and sleepy and afraid to go home, so he just huddled up in the dark theatre until one of his sibling found him there and marched him home. The rest of the story I don't remember. It was a long time ago.

So, whenever I see pictures of the beaches of Hawaii or the tributes to our heroes who died there, I often think of my Hawaiian Dollar. I wished I had framed it. Brother Owen would have been proud of me.

ALMOST LEFT OUT

As the youngest of eight, the last four being boys, I missed out on some things in life. The house I was born in sat atop a bluff with a steep slope leading down to a dirt road winding through the valley. The brothers had to seek their own entertainment during those depression years, and one of the challenges was to back an old farm wagon down the hill as far as they could without losing it, then pull it back up. It didn't take much to entertain them. Three of my brothers, each two years apart in age, did this day after day without anything happening. The idea was to go a little further each day. One day the three of them were working for a record when the older brother slipped and fell and yelled to the others to let go. The brother just two years older than me didn't hear, didn't understand, or didn't care, he held on. He had a reputation as a hardhead. The wagon gained speed, hit something that caused the wagon to flip, and when it did it flipped my brother into the air. When the dust settled the wagon was upside down in the ravine and my brother was beside it unhurt. He wasn't very happy with his brothers. Needless to say, my parents put an end to that game. I don't know if the wagon was salvageable or not.

I wasn't always left out though. A couple of years later they introduced me to smoking. Down in the corn field they would take dried corn silk and a piece of a Ward's catalog and light up. They didn't want me there but figured if I smoked with them I wouldn't tell on them. Their ploy didn't work.

THE VALUE OF PORK

I have never been to Palestine, and at this late date in life I don't expect I ever will be, but I have lived in Canaan. After the family lost the home farm in the depression they moved to Canaan where dad continued to tenant farm. In fact, my dad borrowed a truck and brought mom's sister and her family to Canaan back from Arkansas, but they all soon learned it was not the land of milk and honey of biblical times. It was nice to have family near, but I don't have any memories of those years. This is just what I have been told.

My older siblings do have memories though and our families grew up together and developed life-long strong bonds. We spent a lot of time together over the years because our mothers were such close sisters. In fact, by the middle 1940's we all ended up in Paris where we spent most of the rest of our years of our youth.

Dad told me about the incident with the pig. Aunt Goldie had a son six months older than me and we spent many days and nights in each other's company as children. We didn't have store bought games, but with a few marbles or a deck of cards, we could entertain ourselves through many a winter day and night. Dad tells about the Canaan days when the opportunity arose to weigh Gerald and me on a real scale. At the same time they weighed a small pig. All three of us weighed fifty pounds. Needless to say the pork was more valuable to them at that time than we were because we survived and the pig didn't.

By the time we were fifteen I would outweigh Gerald by a considerable amount, and the pig may survived and I may not have been so lucky if times had not improved. Gerald still survives in Phoenix with his lovely wife Sharon and I've escaped the platter so far here in Southern Illinois.

THE BATTLES WE FOUGHT

If you ever have the opportunity to visit Oakland, Illinois, be sure and go to the town square where I'm sure the old First World War cannon still sits. You'll find it on the southeast corner pointing towards the southeast as it was in days gone by. about seventy that I can attest to. It's only now that I blame some of the older guys in our youthful boy hood army for the duration of W.W.II. Each day, and sometimes more than twice a day, we would mount that cannon and fight the enemy, Germany, with all our strength. I did not understand then that we were firing in the wrong direction. We were lobbing our cannon shots toward Africa; it seems to me when they should have gone toward Berlin. All of our efforts that helped so little in the war effort. Those guys should have known better. I was only a first grader. You may make fun of my foolishness in thinking we could help with that old cannon. Well, the adults had black outs so the enemy planes couldn't see our town at night. If their airplanes could fly that far then, who is to say how far we could lob a cannon shot.

After the war, I teamed up with a different set of neighborhood boys, but we still fought on. We didn't have a cannon in Paris, Illinois to work with, but we had even better weapons. In addition to the cap guns, we had rubber guns and sling shots. The latter two could sting you pretty good. The really handy guys could fix a rubber gun to shoot more than one shot at a time. We had to be a little more careful with the sling shots made with the fork of a small limb, rubber, and the good old tongue out of a worn out shoe. It could fire a small or a large stone. Bee Bee guns weren't allowed in our army as maybe only one existed, and that would be unfair. Kinda like an A Bomb. If you were really lucky you might even have a holster for your cap gun. That was important when you were riding your horse that could have a name of your choice but usually looked like a mop stick or a tree limb.

Most of our battles were now in the badlands and often it was against the Indians. The badlands was on the backside of the cemetery. It was ideal. No one cared that we invaded it and it not only had scrub brush and dwarf trees, but a stream running right down the middle of it which you could leap across in places with your horse and weapons. It was a big place and saw plenty of action. It had some bluffs and hills and hiding places for ambushes and the whole bit. The Saturday afternoon matinees could have been made there. In fact, some of us at times were Gene and Roy and some of the other heroes. I remember when Whip Wilson became a B movie favorite. I liked that fine because I had a big Willow tree in my yard which made dandy whips.

I really don't understand how our steeds held up with all that fighting and running day after day. Sometimes the legs did tire and we couldn't always clear the river, but it wasn't deep. After a rain it would sometimes get unmanageable, but most of the time it was just a steady stream. I'm not sure when we found out that we were playing in the area that the local sewerage emptied in to. Maybe it did smell some, but what sweaty kid doesn't. After fully understanding the circumstances, the battle ground was permanently moved to the County Cemetery and neighboring yards. If the Indians wanted that territory, we'd just make it a reservation.

TOWN VERSUS COUNTRY

I've been torn between two life styles all my life. Am I country or am I an urban boy? Why do I have the conflict? I only spent five and a half years in the country before the family moved to town. After that, most of my years were spent in small towns. How did the dirt get in my veins so early? I have few memories of those years so why does it seem that I'm drawn to the land.

The memories I do have are of catching lightning bugs and using them as night lights before there were electric lights. The fun and games in the yards, fields, and barns and climbing on an old steel wheeled tractor is still in my memory. I'm told my older siblings used to fight over the raisins that were handed out by the government, and they would carry them around in their pockets. I remember the house with absolutely no paint or white wash on it. I remember the garage that my sister Edna pulled me upon to escape our dog when he went mad. I remember the many tin lids nailed to the floor to keep the rodents out. Things in the summer were dusty, dirty, and sweaty all the time.

I had one strong dislike about where we lived in the Bell School District. Four of my siblings attended that school, but I was never allowed to attend the country school. I think I was mistreated. The dislike though had nothing to do with the school. To go to town to Church required that we cross a branch of the Embarrass River. It wasn't a long bridge, but it only had cross planks, no runners. That meant that the wheels hit each individual plank causing it to make a noise. That rattle would scare me silly, I dreaded every trip. There was a longer way to town which would have helped, but with the gas and the war and the rationing of everything, we took the noisy route.

When I just turned five we moved to town. We moved into the biggest house I had ever seen. To me it seemed like a palace. My brother and I actually had our own room. No more three and four in a bed for then. We had free run of the small community of one thousand people and many interesting things to see. It had a 9 cent movie theatre and a park. We didn't get to stay in the big house very long, but I enjoyed my stay there. Our next house was tiny and it was back to four to a bedroom again. That didn't last too long though and by the time I got to start school we were back in a big old unpainted two story house. At least we had space. We moved on when I started the second grade and never looked back. No more country living. When I was eleven I lived for two years in a house in the country, two miles from the nearest town. I loved that. That had to last me until 1984 when this old man of forty seven at the time talked his bride into moving to two acres in the country where they stayed for ten years. The question still exists, Town or Country?

TEACHERS, I'VE HAD A FEW

Next to our parents, teachers have shaped our lives more than we'll ever realize. Think back to those earliest ones that you spent months on end with. There were twenty or thirty kids in a classroom with one adult all day. I loved them all, well almost all. Other teachings has taught me that I need love everybody, but that great teacher knows my heart and I can't lie either. So I will say almost all.

There was Mrs. Lippencott, Mrs. Louise Ring, Mrs. Good, Miss Louise Beall, Miss Mae McClain, Miss Ruth Beall, Mr. Leon Carpenter and the Glithero sisters, and Mrs. Malone. These represent teachers for every year from the first to the eighth grade. Their images are still embedded in my mind. I had two other teachers in my second grade year, but that period was only for five months and they are forgotten.

Two of the above were also principals of the schools. They were also the disciplinarians who I had special attention from. They would tell me I was too loud and pushing others around was not the way to go. They took the time because I was a good student in the classroom, but when they exited the room for any reason I took over generally. My voice changed early and I didn't realize how it would carry down the halls until they called me on it. I won't say I changed overnight, but it did make an impact.

Everyone has a favorite and for me that was Mrs. Good. The name fit her well. What a sweet personality she had. She was very plain as looks go, but her encouragement and kind words made you want to be in her class and excel if possible. Back then they didn't call them Parent Teacher conferences, but parent were all invited to the classroom and Mrs. Good chose me to sing publicly for the first time. "Yo Ho, Blow the Man Down" I'm sure I made quite an impression on the parents.

The Beall sisters of my fourth and sixth years were no nonsense dedicated teachers. They lived together in an impressive brick home not too far from the school, and the sixth grade teacher was also the principal. They were both about five foot tall and a little on the hefty side. They could smile a little, but not much. I thought them to be fair and impartial to all the students.

Mae McClain was probably my second favorite teacher. She was the biggest teacher in the elementary school and the jolliest. She loved to laugh and it was a joy to be in her classroom. Remembering her classroom was to see students lining the wall in the order that they could spell. It was an ongoing competition and it was difficult to get to the head of the line with all of those smart girls.

Mr. Carpenter, the only man, was my teacher and my coach. I can't remember anything he ever taught me in the classroom, but I spent a lot of time on the basketball court with him. The Glithero sisters took care of most of the teaching. We had a good group of boys and in my eighth grade we won the County Basketball Tournament. That was the year that Mrs. Malone taught us. She was a happy older teacher, probably about fifty, who didn't appear to be as dedicated as some, but we liked her.

That leaves Miss Louise Ring, my second grade teacher. Well at least that is where I finished my second grade. I only had her for two months, but she made an impression. I started my second grade in 1944 in Oakland, Illinois. I passed on from Miss Lippencott's first grade but had barely found a seat when the family moved to Decatur where my dad was working. Though it was only sixty miles, in the war years you could only get so much gas and replacement tires, so sixty miles was a long way. Things changed again and we moved eighty miles to Paris, Illinois in April of 1945, just in time for me to meet my new classmates that I would stick with for the next four years, and Miss Ring. I'm thinking maybe she didn't like kids from Decatur. Was I ever happy when June came and school was out.

School days. In a family where my siblings have had a difficult time remembering in the last years of their lives, memories are so precious. Even if they do include the black haired lady with a sprinkling of grey in her hair and the cold black stare. I'm sure I probably learned something from her too.

EARLY SCHOOL SYSTEMS

In Coles County, Illinois when there were still many country schools, each district would be given a name. My father attended the Yellow Hammer School in his youth as did several of my siblings. Some children had the same teacher for most of their youth. It just so happened that the only teacher dad remembered was the mother of a shop teacher that I had in high school forty years later. My siblings attended the

Yellow Hammer School District, then the Canaan District before moving to the Bell District and then on to schools in Oakland. I was the only one that did not get to attend a rural school.

Policies could be quite flexible in these districts. My sister Edna completed her fourth grade and then the following years, because there was no one else in her fifth grade class, she had to repeat the fourth grade. My brother Dale was due to start the first grade along with two other boys when the district lost its teacher. They were then transported to town where they were not well received. They didn't fit in and the teacher failed all three of them. The following year the District had a teacher again so they were to start over again as first graders. The teacher quickly realized that they didn't belong there and advanced them to the second grade. My older sister Eula decided that she was old enough and didn't want to go to school anymore. My parents tried to convince her to stay in school and she finally relented if she could take my brother Cleo with her. He was a year too young to start school, but arrangements were made and he started one year early.

I'm not sure if that benefitted my brother as he was always the smallest in his class and had big sister hanging over him and protecting him in a one room school. How could this have happened? It didn't hurt that my dad was on the school board. That was logical because of the twenty or so pupils in the one room school, five of them were his. Policies were flexible then.

IT TRULY FELT LIKE HOME

Living in six different places in eight years, it was a little difficult to feel at home. We always had our parents and siblings but the next move was just around the corner. That's the way it was when we left Oakland to go to Decatur to be closer to Dad's work in the defense industry. To start school in September in Oakland and then move by the end of October wasn't ideal. It was a big change going to a big city and entering big schools. In the process we left brother Dale behind. He had started High School and decided he'd stay in Oakland and work for some men there and drop out of school. The rest of us consisting of sister Eula and her baby daughter Donna, sister Edna, and we three younger boys settled in a tri-plex housing unit built for the defense workers. Ours was a 3 bedroom unit on one end of the building, sitting next to hill leading down to an Interurban Rail line. Looked like a trolley track to me, but I'm no transportation expert. Here we had modern utilities. Loved it! At school Aaron and I were put in the slow learner's classroom because we didn't have much of a record to go on. After a couple of weeks we were advanced to the accelerated class. That and the fact that we had fun sliding down the hill on boxes and tin are about all I can share about that. We always posted a look out at the bottom to warn when a train was coming. I'm sure we all have scars from those days dealing with metal and tracks.

The two little blond girls living next door to me let me play paper dolls with them. That was about the time that the song "Paper Dolls" made it big. I never became very proficient at it as in April we moved again to Paris, Illinois. Perhaps had we stayed in Decatur longer I would have learned more about the female species and how to treat them.

On our way to Paris we picked brother Dale up again so we had nine of us living in a neat little four room house with a large side yard and a white picket fence. I don't know the details on why the quick move, but I do know it turned out for the best. We had no in house conveniences, but the well was just outside the kitchen door. The two seater outhouse was back beyond the grape harbor. There was a beautiful willow tree in the middle of the yard which sort of divided the side yard from the garden area. In warm weather some of us boys could sleep on the small enclosed back porch with Mom's manual washing machine. After about a year Dad added a bedroom for the three younger boys after Dale had moved out on his own.

The house was situated on a corner one block from the entrance of the County Cemetery. Just kitty cornered from our lot was a new city park under construction. It was probably about a ten acre park with the end closest to us being the prettiest. They had planted trees, bushes, and flowers and highlighted it all with a wading pool. The other end had the ball diamond, the kid and big swings, the sand box, and the basketball goals along with various and sundry other activities. We felt like we had just died and gone to heaven.

As we were entering the warmer weather we soon got to know the kids. Our closest neighbors were Junior and Ronny Ryan. Almost within a stone's throw we had the four Givens children, Frank, Patty, Beverly, and Bozo. Bozo's real name was Orville Lee, but to us he will always be Bozo. Next to them lived the Utterbacks, Junior and Ella Mae. Ella Mae was a classmate of mine. For the next four years we had a lot of fun and got into a lot of mischief with the group. We fought and we made up and we shared toys. Mainly we shared Junior Ryan's toys, he had the most and you wouldn't believe the comic book collection that he had and the most marbles of anyone in the neighborhood. Many of them won off of me. For a couple of years most of the younger ones of the group spent hours in the wading pool and there we shared sun burns and nasty sores. We had never had it so good. We always showed up at home for meals, but otherwise we had plenty going on. We were at home.

THE NEIGHBORHOOD

There were kids all over the place in the area of the Sunrise Park in my youth, but there was just so many that you got really tight with. Our large city block fulfilled that requirement for us. When you got right down to it, there were eleven kids in my age group in our old neighborhood. From that group you could immediately eliminate Mary Jo, the Cemetery Trustee's daughter. She was the prettiest of the bunch but was above our social class.

Remaining were our nearest neighbors, the Ryans. Elmer Junior Horace Ryan was my brother Aaron's age. We didn't call him Elmer nor did we consistently call him Junior. As often as not we called him like his mother did when she'd say, 'Elmer Junior Horace Ryan, you get home.' His younger brother was Ronny. Although Ronny was just a year younger than me, he was different. He walked around very quietly with a shy smile. He didn't get involved in our marble games. He'd just sit and watch for hours. He would get his six shooters and gallop around with the rest of us, but a lot of time he was just the spectator and we respected that. No one picked on Ronny.

Behind them sat the Givens household. Frank the older was not about to play with the kids, but the other three did, depending on what we were playing. Patty the oldest would play hide and seek with us at night if my older brother Cleo was playing. It seems they spent a lot of time hiding in the Cemetery that was just across the street from our block. Beverly was about game for anything and was pretty bossy. Orville Lee the younger was one little pest. He was the youngest of the group and everyone called him Bozo.

Back toward the rear of our house was Junior and Ella Mae Utterback. If that sounds like they came from the hills of Kentucky, I think they must have. They looked like it, dressed like it, and talked like it. Junior was the toughest in the neighborhood and Ella Mae was in my class at school. Junior had the most sophisticated weapons and two pair of boxing gloves that he liked to get someone to spar with him. We'd prefer he not show up, but he often did and pushed us around pretty good. The Swinford boys decided it was time to call his bluff and decided to teach him a lesson. He was being his usual self one day when Aaron dived and got a hold of one leg and Cleo and I were to take him down. At that time we had a change of plans and I took off for home and Cleo deserted Aaron also. We decided we needed a new plan.

Older brother Dale was still home but he had bigger fish to fry until we told him of our problem with Junior Utterback. Now Junior was quite the boxer because his brother was in the Navy and boxed there. He didn't hesitate when Dale asked him to put on the gloves with him. It didn't take long for the street fighter to teach the boxer a few tricks and our war was won. Junior quit bothering us, most of the time. I don't know why Dale did that because he let us know quite often that he didn't like us.

That was our group. We played a lot of hide and seek. Without sounding conceded I have to say that Ella Mae was sweet on me, but the feeling wasn't mutual. The guys played a lot of marbles and westerns and wars. Junior and Ronny had the store bought six shooters and dozens of comic books, but we had the largest arsenal of sling shots and rubber guns. Even though rubber was rationed, tire tubes didn't last forever. I wish I had a dime for every marble that I lost in games with Elmer Junior Hoarce Ryan. Whether it was big circle marbles or little circle marbles, he seemed always to have the superior shooters, even steelies, although we tried to outlaw them. Ball bearing were pretty plentiful when the older guys were doing a lot of car overhauls in the side yard.

These are the guys that taught me about the birds and bees. Parents just assumed you'd learn about those things the same way they did back then, by being stung a few time. I can truthfully say there were no experts in our crowd. The girls shared what they knew, they weren't bashful about it. The guys were a little more sneaky. We peeked in windows but in one case I know Beverly did the same. We left town when I was twelve and I lost touch with the old neighborhood. When I returned two years later many of them had disappeared.

IT'S ALL ABOUT THE BALL

I don't remember having any interest in the ball until I made the move to Paris where the schools introduced me to the game of dodge ball and shooting at a hoop nailed to a tree. The ball used was the same. It was a round rubber looking bladder. I'm sure we wore out many of them. Some of the boys had personal ball gloves, bats, and a ball that we also played after school. That game would last until the owner of the ball had to go home. Somewhere along the line one of the guys got a pig skin, a real football. As I recall I was about ten and it didn't take long to catch on. Organized mayhem. You could beat up on each other and not get in trouble. Well most of the time.

We had enough guys interested that after school we could go about a half block north and play on the front lawn of U.O. Colsons, the big business that made calendars and advertising stuff, and lord who knows what else. They had a beautiful lawn and it also had attractive shrubs to beautify the property also. Whether we had six guys show up to play or fifteen, we always played as long as the boy who owned the ball could stay. The fall of my sixth grade it didn't take long before the wear and tear on that beautiful lawn began to show. The bushes kept us well clear of the windows and the bushes stayed healthy, but the grass had met its challenge. Despite all this, the good people at U.O. Coulson's never ran the football players off. They weren't as lenient with the softball/baseball group, but the football players stayed the course until the winter drove them inside.

Someone came up with the idea of challenging the other schools in town to games for the following spring. To my knowledge no adults were even involved in the communication between Vance (my school) and Redman, Mayo, or Tanner. As it turned out Mayo didn't want to participate but three of the four did. In fairness, Mayo was a part of the school that included the Junior High and they may have already had an opportunity to enter the Junior High program in some way. The remaining three set up a schedule and got permission to play on the High School Field. We were restricted to the end zone and the first ten yards out and we were ecstatic that we were playing where the big boys played, but we didn't get to use the lights. This was all long before the High Schoolers started spring sessions.

You have to understand the layout of the Paris School System. Vance School was the northernmost school and in today's lingo it would be called the white collar section of town. The Redman School was the southernmost school and in my estimation would be considered the blue collar section of town. Then there was the Tanner School in the West End that I was almost afraid to ride my bike through, and it was the Red collar section as far as I was concerned. That was long before I ever heard of a red-neck. In hindsight I think the boys represented their sections well.

This inner-city play was probably the first of its kind in Paris. I know my older brother did not participate in any such contests, so my class was the first to contend for the elementary championship of Paris. Now Paris was a community of ten thousand people, so that is no small accomplishment. It was a historical undertaking. Our uniforms resembled very closely the cloths that we wore to school on any particular game day and helmets did not exist. There was no need for flags as this was tackle ball, not pretend football. This nose that I have struggled with all my life is proof that we were just not playing around. In our last game against Redman, I not only got tackled but a second guy landed on me driving my beak into the hard ground. After the blood flow was stopped, my brother took me home. He had probably been one or the only referee. We didn't pay well. When Dad examined my nose and black eyes the next morning, he recalls me asking him if I could play football when I got to High School. I did despite my mother's fear that I would get hurt. Maybe if I had realized how sick she was I would have forgone my desire, but she lived through my first two high school years of football, and I didn't get hurt. On the other hand, my brother Aaron played basketball during that same period and broke his collar bone in two places.

I don't remember who won the non-existent trophy that inaugural year, but I am pretty sure it was not the White Collar School. Maybe the season didn't finish. Maybe the owner of the ball just went home.

HAVE YOU EVER?

We've all shared many of life's experiences. But have you ever:

On snowy roads hooked onto the back bumper of a slow moving automobile for a ride, with or without a sled.

Stolen a watermelon from a field on a hot day and eaten its lush red contents.

Turned over an outhouse on Halloween.

Kneeled down in the dirt shooting marbles so much as to wear a hole in the knee of your pants.

Caught a hundred lightning bugs and put them into a ventilated quart jar.

Played in a hay mow (loft to some) of a barn in the hay and straw.

Played hide and go seek in a cemetery.

Gone swimming in a pool with sores on your body bigger than a silver dollar.

Stubbed your toes so badly that they took a week to heal.

Made ice cream using newly fallen snow.

Worn shoes when the only sole you had was a piece of cardboard.

Picked up coal along the railroad tracks to keep you house warm.

Followed the pickers in the corn field to recover the fallen corn to make a few dollars.

Made homemade ice cream with a manual ice cream maker.

Road on the handlebars of a bicycle.

Been greased down with vapor rub, chest and back to combat a cold.

Taken kerosene and sugar to fight congestion.

Played in the snow until you were soaked and wet to your skin.

Hiked a mile in a snow storm.

Hitch hiked to catch a ride as a kid.

Cleaned out chicken houses and hog houses to make a few bucks.

Stolen candy from the corner grocery store.

Lied to parents, teachers, authorities to escape punishment.

Cheated on test, school or otherwise.

Have you ever given your solemn word to a friend, and then broken it.

Slid down a slope on a piece of tin and have the scar to show for it.

Used your sleeve or bare arm for a hanky when you didn't have one, or maybe even when you did.

Gotten smashed at a Worlds Fair.

Bought a used car and have the engine blow up the first time you drive it out of town.

Played Goliath as an adult in a church youth production.

Had a bald headed Canary.

Has written two novels that are available on line. "If We Never Meet Again This Side of Heaven", and "Because of Mother's Prayer", a sequel.

Did any shameful advertising.

I'm not saying I ever did any of these, but it makes you think. You could probably add quite a list to this one. No one's perfect.

PARK CAN MEAN DIFFERENT THINGS

I won't even try to answer the questions that the title may bring. Each reader has their own experiences to draw on. Let's just say that my parent's move to Paris, Illinois in 1945 with three kids, still in the elementary school grades, could not have impacted their lives more. That move, within fifty feet of a city park, changed them immensely. That park brought the whole neighborhood youth together in a very special way. Somehow and for some reason the leaders of the community had managed during the war years to plan for the future by building two new parks, and the Sunrise Park in the east end of Paris was the latest. For over four years this proved to be a blessing for us.

Across town was the Sunset Park. Not as nice as ours but pleasant. In the South end of town was the Sylvian Park. That one always confused me a little as it was smaller. It had a water tower in one corner and the main attraction was benches. It was an older park and I guess they thought parks were for sitting and feeding the pigeons back in the thirties. Close by the Sylvian was an elementary school with a large play yard, and each end of town had one of those so there was no shortage of space to have fun. The school yards were never closed to the public and it was rare to see a blade of grass grow on any of them. Paris did it one better though. On the far north end of town they had the Twin Lakes Park. A large recreational area surrounded on two sides by water. In addition to the green landscape and the trees, in the forties there was a beach with piers, diving boards, floats, and life guards. You could rent boats and entertain yourself in the dance hall pavilion and games combination at lake side. It was a popular area for the kids.

Twin Lakes Park was also a convenient place for large family reunions down under the trees. The Park Commission furnished big picnic tables and trash bins and areas for horse shoe pitching and electricity for hooking up lights, amplifiers, and the like. The Swinford Family adopted it early on and in the late forties would have in excess of 200 family members down under the trees having a grand old time. In the fifties the Park Commission built a large pavilion in the middle of the Park which kept the people dry and more comfortable in varying types of weather. That same pavilion will be used in 2017 for the 100th. Anniversary of the Swinford Family Reunion, Lord willing.

I digress. The other part of the Twin Lakes sits east of the main highway running through the community and they are joined at the water works by only a narrow passage of water. There wasn't much going on in that part of the lake in the forties and fifties. At the far eastern side it had a Dam that controlled the release of the water to the countryside. Further north there was an area that people could pull their car down to and wash it, or take a swim. Town's people had a name for it but I can't recall what it was. This and the dam were popular with primarily the guys that couldn't afford the fees at the pay beach. We visited that area quite often. Less visited was the Dam area because it was deeper and more dangerous. There was no shallow water there. It was a little closer to our home though. Maybe that's why my two older brothers stopped there one day and went skinny dipping. I, a non-swimmer, was left sitting on the concrete reinforcements that reached out into the deeper part of the lake. Whether the concrete was mossy or just wet, and whether I had any cloths on or not, I began slipping out into the deeper water and was having trouble catching hold and stopping my slide. My brothers made a mad dash from the Dam area where they were swimming and between them and some weeds I caught on to, I'm still around to tell the tale. They made me promise not to tell mom and dad and I didn't, until I got home. I don't remember ever going to the Dam again with them.

But again I stray. Until I finished the sixth grade I became acquainted with every park and every school yard in Paris. What a joy it was to have grown up in a community with ten thousand people and four or five nice parks. I still love to drive pass the Sunrise Park. It's still beautiful. The wading pool has been concreted in now, but in the late forties I spent many hours there, especially after the Dam incident. I'd be surprised if the kids used the public parks much anymore with so much going on in their lives. With their cell phones, televisions, computers, and many other games and things available the parks must look pretty dull. You don't see children riding broom sticks and playing cowboy and Indians anymore and using their imagination as much. Times have changed. Who is to say which is the better.

MARY, WHERE ARE YOU NOW?

In the sixth grade, my brother Aaron was many things. He was probably the best looking with his blonde hair and blue eyes on his tall torso. The girls really liked him. I had not gotten old enough to be envious of him, yet. He could run and play ball with the best of them and I'm sure was one of the smartest kids in his class. Yes, he had lots of things going for himself, but he also had a drawback or two. Beside the head as hard as a rock, he was as stubborn as a mule too, and would rather fight than change his mind or admit he might be wrong. I had lived with that for years, but some of the guys in his class just had not gotten used to it. Because of that, the fighting came all too often. If more than two confronted him, I was expected to cover his back and I tried to do my part. He could normally handle two. I was on a different side of the playground so I couldn't always be there for him. One day he took it to a higher level. He told one of his classmates that his little brother could lick him and the kid took him up on it.

Now you have to understand that this was before all of these video games, karate and all such things. A licking was a take down and ending up on top and the guy couldn't get up. Oh we'd punch arms sometimes, but I never struck anyone in the face as a youth. So just off the playground after school I took Estes Johnson down, and got a reputation for doing it. It's true that he was at least 2 years older and bigger than I, but what they didn't know was I had been fighting with boys 2 and 4 years older than I all my life. My brothers. I was no amateur. For the next year that reputation held and I wasn't really tested too many times. When Billy Sunkel came to town from the country school to my class, he was taller but when some of the guys wanted him to challenge me, he passed. The only blood drawn in my grade school years was when Donny Knoepfel did something I didn't like and I threatened him. Donny was a good friend of mine and when he threw up his arms to defend himself, he bloodied my lip.

I was never mean, but I wanted to be liked and if being the king of the roost would help me, that is what I'd be. The principal more than once told me that was the wrong way when I got an invitation to her private room, but I had to learn it for myself. First clue was when I wanted to be Captain of the Patrol Boys my 6th. Grade. That was an elected position by the class and I lost to Donny Knoepfel. I found that even the cute little girls seem to prefer some of the curly headed shrimps instead of me. I was beginning to get the message, but it didn't come overnight. I did well in the classroom, but was a mighty slow learner in other ways.

A new student came to our school in the 6th.Grade also. Her name was Mary Martha Mitchell. Mary came with a certain air about her that one didn't want to challenge. She wasn't one of the cute little girls so I had no reason to try and impress her so I just kept my distance, and she did too. She was about the same height as me and probably outweighed me. I'm not sure, but I think she must have had an older brother or father into weight lifting because she had a set of arms on her. Before that year was over I found out that while I might rule the roost, she owned the chicken house and she didn't so much as have to flex a muscle. First, I knew I could never fight a woman, and secondly I know that I didn't want to fight Mary Martha Mitchell. Her stare clearly instructed one and all that they were not to mess with her. When I got that message, we got along okay. I think she even kind of liked me a little. She defeated me with attitude and never laid a glove on me.

After elementary school my family moved and I started over in a new school that didn't know that I was supposed to be the King of the Roost, so I didn't let on. It was a happy two years but Aaron just got more handsome and the girls still preferred him. At the end of those two years we moved back to Paris again and I started High School. It didn't cross my mind immediately, but eventually I noted that Mary Martha was not in the Freshmen Class. She had moved. It meant I wouldn't have to walk the halls with one eye looking out for her. To this day I don't know what happened to Mary Martha. Mary, where are you now?

THE FABULOUS FIVE

Edgar County, Illinois is located just 150 miles south of Chicago on the Indiana border. The County Seat is Paris with a population in 1950 of ten thousand people. Paris was known in the thirties, forties and fifties for its high school basketball teams, winning the state championship twice and multiple seconds and thirds against much more populated areas, under the coaching of Coach Ernie Eveland.

This isn't about Paris though, as fabulous as they might have been. Edgar County also has smaller communities with populations at that time of less than two thousand people. Each of these communities had basketball also at the high school and junior high school levels. These schools numbered six in all and they competed against each other for the title of County Champion each year. Paris did not participate with this group as they had bigger fish to fry, but none the less the towns of Kansas, Redman, Brocton, Hume/Metcalf, Chrisman and Scotland took the competition very seriously.

This story is about the fabulous five Chrisman Junior High basketball team of 1950. With Coach Leon Carpenter, they conducted an unbeaten season playing each county team twice and probably two smaller non county teams also. At the end of the regular schedule there was then a tournament to determine the Edgar County Junior High Champions, with the exception of the Paris team of course. The junior high team of Chrisman won that tournament with forwards Gene Ryan and Bob Browning, center Luther Colter, and guards Carrol Calhoun and Donald Swinford, with team members Richard Swank and Freddie Cavanaugh contributing. That team picture published by the Paris Beacon News no doubt hangs in infamy somewhere. I know it's in my keepsakes.

Apparently someone thought that a game should be set up between the fabulous five of Chrisman and the Mayo Tigers of Paris, Illinois. Of course we couldn't wait to get there and play them on their home court and we drew a large crowd. Everyone wanted to see the little guys beat the big city boys. At least the county people did. It was a terrific competitive game all the way, but dreams come to an end and we lost to Paris by less than 4 points. We were down cast, but proud.

The following year I had moved to Paris and played with the same guys that had just beaten my team the season before.

The nucleus of that team, class of 1955, went on to the Sweet Sixteen Illinois High School Basketball play offs. They didn't win, but the fabulous five of Chrisman Junior high did Chrisman proud to compete so well against the big boys of Edgar County. I'm sure it's a memory that we'll never forget and have told our children over and over. I'm still in touch with Ryan and Colter and we still talk about it. Can't blame a guy for remembering those happy times, can you? We each got a blue C about four inches high trimmed in yellow. I don't know what ever happened to mine.

RED DELICIOUS TOMATOES

If God made one perfect food stuff, this is it, tomatoes. I would like to think the vines were all over the Garden of Eden, and should have been all that Adam and Eve desired. What a beautiful world we could have had if they had eaten the fruit of the vine instead the fruit of the tree. I know some of you are going to point out that the tomato is not a fruit. Well to me it will always surpass any fruit on this planet.

Not only is the tomato delicious, it is a product of commerce. People in the country grow it for the people in the city that also love them and large operations that make tomato products. That creates work for the country people like my kind growing up. It was my first effort to earn income when I was about seven years old in 1944. I wanted that money for movies, sodas, candy and popcorn. The older siblings didn't want to fool with me but I tagged along anyway. It was just a short two mile walk out into the country.

When we got there I saw a huge field of vines with bright red tomatoes growing on them. What a beautiful sight. At the sides of the field were crates to be filled with the tomatoes and you got money for doing just that. The man in charge no doubt looked at me with some skepticism, but he told me to write my name on each crate I filled, and at the end of the day I would get paid. We were each given a row to work and off we went. I was slower than my siblings and they soon out distanced me. I didn't count on the heat of the summer or the weight of the crate as it filled up, but for a while I worked diligently at picking the ripe fruit vine by vine and moving on. When the crate was full you'd carry or drag it back to the end of the row to be picked up.

It wasn't long before I was exhausted and had to sit down after dragging that heavy thing back to the end of the row. I carefully wrote my name on the side of the crate and took my time recovering. There were several crates that had not been picked up and put on the truck along the field. How easy it was to just erase the name in chalk on them and replace it with my own. I had about all this labor that I could take, so when no one was looking I did my deed. I wouldn't be greedy, just a few. I apparently did one to many and was spotted by someone who told on me and I got fired. I was told to go home and I didn't even collect for what I had done. It was a long walk home without any change for a cold soda or candy.

Mom and Dad always had big gardens with lots of tomatoes. The thought of biting into the big red ones and having the juices running down my cheeks still makes me feel good. I liked a little salt, but I'd take them anyway I could find them. Many a time a piece of buttered bread wrapped around a green onion and several tomatoes made for a wonderful snack or lunch. I wasn't as fond of weeding the garden but I did what I had to do to enjoy those tomatoes. In addition, Mom would always can quart after quart of them for the winter time. They never lasted long enough. She didn't make a lot of sauces like the ladies do now. It was mainly just tomatoes in a bowl and often breaded tomatoes.

When I retired and took my social security I got a list of my contributions made by the year. Sure enough, there as the first item in 1950 was my first paying job. It was a job planting, picking, and hauling tomatoes. The memory has not dimmed. The farmer, Spencer Fortune, hired us boys to help set several acres of tomatoes just down the road from where we lived when I was thirteen. We'd sit on the planter and space the plants at given intervals as it was pulled along by the tractor. The planter would shoot out a spurt of water at those intervals and a hoe would pull in the dirt around the set. We only stopped for more settings or when the water tank need refilled. Unlike my first job in the tomato fields, I must have done something right as a beautiful field of tomatoes was grown and Mr. Fortune came back and hired us for the harvest.

This time my brother Aaron and I were hired to load the tomatoes and take them to market. It was our job to put the crates on the truck and when it was loaded we'd ride up top when the trucker took them into town to be unloaded. During that trip, we could eat all of the tomatoes we could hold, and for me that was saying a lot. I looked forward to that ride to town with the wind blowing on our sweaty body, eating tomatoes. For that we got paid and the job went on for two or three days, and Uncle Sam deducted social security from our earnings. Without that job, my social security at retirement would have been smaller. Every $32.00 earning counted.

But, that's not the end of that story. I probably should not tell that my brother may have thrown a few tomatoes mashed in the loading at passing cars. Not me, I would eat them. I was a good boy. I ate lots more tomatoes than him. That is no doubt why I ended up with the largest hives ever recorded in the Swinford family. I had them everywhere. It seems that Mr. Fortune sprayed those tomatoes during the growing season with some kind of chemical that I didn't know about. Sure didn't hurt the flavor, but those hives stayed around a considerable length of time.

Every summer since I've grown tomatoes or headed out to find a farmer's market early on with lots of red tomatoes. Some years when I grew them I couldn't even wait until they turned red. Even if they had a tint of pink, that was close enough for me. I generally wash them though in case they've been sprayed. You never know. Most years I can never get enough of the delicious fruit. God knew what he was doing when he paired my wife and me up though. He not only gave me a wife but also three children that just aren't that crazy about tomatoes. I'm a lucky man.

I look at it this way. There are many desirable fruits in this world. Adam and Eve have already taken the fall eating of that forbidden tree, so it should be okay for my family to partake of it now and leave my tomatoes to me. Hot house tomatoes, Ugh, but better than nothing.

NEWS ON YOUR DOORSTEP

'Neither wind, rain, snow, sleet, nor dark of night will keep us from making our appointed rounds' may be the motto adhered to by the Post Office in years gone by. You'll notice I've indicated it must be a past motto. Paper boys could go them one better. The paper would get delivered the same day even if the press broke down.

Paris Beacon News was a publication delivered every day but Sunday to the subscribers in the community of 10,000 people of Paris, Illinois. They used a superior group of young boys (no girls in the late forties) to see that the customers got their important reading material. I know, because I was one, standing tall proud to serve. One summer the company even took us to Chicago on a bus to see the Cubs and Pirates play. They wanted to treat us right.

Normally the minimum age was twelve to qualify for this auspicious job. The age restriction would sometimes be relaxed, as it was in my case, because I was either such a hot prospect or the fact that I already had two brothers delivering who had good working reputations.

The location of the newspaper's business was just a half block off of the city square, not far from the Court House. The front faced Main Street with the offices for management and all of the sales people and reporters. Behind on the alley was that section with the presses and print set-up department along with paper storage. There really wasn't any place for the fine carriers, but in wet or bad weather they would let us cram into the back by the storage. Normally we'd wait out by the back dock where our allotment of papers would be brought out to us. Most of the routes involved bundles of 80 to a 100 papers which was about all one person could fold and deliver safely and timely on a bicycle.

When you were hired, two things happened. First, you were given the route book which had a page for each customer on your route. It showed name and address, and had about 30 tear off sections showing the date. About every 6 months you would get new inserts for your books. Collections were to be made each Saturday and the stub given the customer showing the date, their receipt. That book was very important and it was impressed on us that this had to be protected. Sometimes customers chose to pay at the office and this was clearly shown in the book. The second thing was you were given a newspaper bag. It was designed to carry the papers and had a flap to keep them dry. It could sit on the front fender of a bicycle and the strap would reach the handle bar grips. If you were lucky you had spinner knobs to wrap the straps around. The office would keep track of how many customers you had and how much you should collect. On Saturday mornings you would make the rounds and then stop in by noon and pay your bill. If there was anything left, you could skip across the street to the ice cream parlor that had the very best milk shakes. Some weeks you came up short and had to delay the shake.

I don't recall the exact price for 6 papers delivered to your door, but it wasn't much. It was surely less than fifty cents. You'd be surprised how many people could not be located on

Saturday morning to pay their bill. You'd have to make stops each evening the following week to try and catch them. I recall for some it would take two or three weeks to catch up with them. Then there were the ones who were at home but had no change. Like a paper boy was going to make change for a twenty dollar bill. This was the weekly battle to make any money. Once in a while you'd meet a sweet little old lady that thought you had beautiful brown eyes or hair like her deceased husband had and you'd collect an extra dime. I made sure I tossed their paper in just the right spot.

The routine was that you'd get your papers at the dock. Then two or three of you would find a spot to sit and fold papers before going to the area of town where your route was. My brother Aaron and I had routes next to each other. We always folded papers together in the vicinity of the 5 cent soda pop at the nearest gas station. I absolutely could not resist dumping a 5 cent bag of Planter's Peanuts into a Coke. The best.

The newspaper was almost always 8 pages and could easily be folded in three sections and those folds into another three sections before stuffing in the edges. It was not uncommon for the guys to have speed races doing it. It wasn't much fun when a 12 page paper was printed and we had to change our style. Most of us did just one threefold and tucked in the edges. It was faster to fold but harder to pack and terrible to try and throw. If you couldn't ride right up to the porch or stoop, you had to walk it up, slowing down everything.

I had helped my brother before I got on as a regular, so I was pretty well acquainted with his route. Over a period of time he learned mine, so that in the case of sickness we could help each other out. The paper might get there late, but it got there. The only real mishap I ever had delivering papers was carrying his route for him. I was riding along slinging papers at the porches right and left when I saw a lady sitting in her chair with her dog. Rather than take a chance on hitting her, I stopped my bicycle and carried the paper up to her. She thanked me very nicely, but when I turned and make a quick exit down off the porch her dog latched onto my thigh with the biggest mouth I'd ever seen. She couldn't get him stopped fast enough and he left one large wound that I carry a scar for today. Of course I had the Tetanus shot and the dog was tested for rabies. We both survived.

I had a good route with friendly people for the most part. The best thing was that I had three Mom and Pop Corner Grocery stores on my route. On days when I had a little collection I could stop at all three and enjoy myself. Usually ten dollars a week would be a big haul when all the dead-beats paid up. That was about sixty cents an hour. Not bad.

I don't recall, but I'm sure Dad had to front the money for the used bicycle I had and all of its upkeep, but at least I had matinee money. Up until two years ago I had paper delivery to my house daily. It came in an automobile. I wonder who fronted the money for their car and do they still make ten dollars. Now I've switched to mail delivery as I'm getting three papers. I don't get them hot off the presses, but they are delivered to my mail box the next day or two, or more. Whatever happened to that motto, 'neither rain, sleet, snow…"

THAT FIRST REAL DATE

Who doesn't remember that first real date? Not the meet you in the malt shop or at the weekly matinee, but a real invitation to go out where you picked them up at their home and made an evening of it. Mine is still pretty vivid.

It wasn't like I didn't know the routine; I'm the youngest of eight. There was no age restriction in our family about when you could start dating. Nature just took its course. One sister married when she was sixteen so you know things were pretty flexible. Starting with about the fourth grade I noticed the girls a lot and thought myself quite dashing. After spin the bottle and post office games I graduated to holding hands in the matinees and sometimes even on hayrides, but no formal dates. Generally I guess that was reserved until you could drive. I guess I was pretty interested in Rae. I don't even know how we met; she didn't go to my school. I only know that we ended up meeting a few times at the matinee and I thought she was special. She was a twin a year younger than me. Then we moved and Rae was gone.

As a freshman in high school I don't even remember speaking to a girl but surely I must have. I certainly didn't have any dates, but I didn't feel out of place, most of the guys I knew weren't dating either. It seemed to be a pattern, all the cute freshman girls liked the older guys and vice versa. Anyway, they weren't missed in my schedule of football, basketball, and track. I managed to keep busy. I'd be an upper classman someday. It wasn't like I couldn't drive. I'd been driving since I was twelve, but it wasn't until late in my freshman year that I had the formality of a driver's license.

My mother was quite ill when I started my sophomore year. She spent most of her time in the hospital or the front bedroom of our home that used to be Aaron and my bedroom. It was in that same bedroom that Aaron, who was dating, first had his heart broken and I sat while he sobbed and wondered why Gwen dumped him. I wondered too. If he had trouble with a girl, what chance would I have? All of this was going on when I saw someone that I never expected to see again. Rae came in with the new crop of freshmen and she seemed as happy to see me as I was her. We didn't see each other much but she always had the greatest smile for me and I was smitten. Whether it was a new picture or an old one, she gave me a picture that I remember rushing home to show my mother as she lay in bed. I remember how she smiled and told me she thought she was very pretty. I kept that picture close to me at all times.

Whether it was the cold spell before my mother passed away in November, or in the cold month afterwards, Aaron encouraged me to get a date with Rae and double date with him. He had bounced back after Gwen and was in the game. It took a while but I finally found the courage to ask and she got permission to go on a double date with me. I don't recall where we went, probably a movie, but I do remember having a cold to end all colds. I was blowing and snorting and couldn't have been very pleasant to be around, but I couldn't cancel a first date. Anyway, she lived in the country and on our way to take her home, brother Aaron decided to stop along the country road not too far from her home for a little getting to know you session. I don't know if that was for me or for him, but all I could do was roll the window down part way so I could breathe. If I tried to kiss her that night, and I don't think I did, it would have been trouble. I was gasping through my mouth for air. Anyway, that was the way the night ended.

I got over the cold, and Rae still smiled at me sweetly, but Rae never again accepted my invitation for a date. By that time the upper classmen, juniors and seniors, had their eyes on her but I don't think they were successful. Years later our paths crossed at a class reunion. She was in the same class as my wife. She had married one of the guys that I played football with. Butch had been up and coming freshmen when I was a senior, so she ended up going for a younger man.

TEENAGE BUDDY

As a kid I like to think that I had many friends. I like people and for the most part they like me, but it's true that you only have so many really close friends, the ones that you can bare your soul to. This was definitely true in my teen years.

I started a new school in my 7th. grade, not knowing a single person in my class. I wasn't exactly lost but was up against groups that had already bonded and even a family of cousins that ruled the roost. My salvation was another guy in the same boat, Luther. We found ourselves together more and more and before you know it we were a pair. He had moved in from Tennessee and talked real funny but we could laugh and cut up and ended up playing a lot of basketball together for our junior high years.

He's the only guy that I remember asking me to come home with him and staying overnight. Of course I didn't know that he had chores until sundown and they were to include me. His dad was a tenant farmer and it was Luther's job to come home after school and pick corn. He taught me everything he knew about picking corn by hand and throwing it into a wagon. I didn't really mind though. We had each other's back against the groups in the class that tried to shove people around and we stood our ground. He was one tough customer, shorter than me but tougher than nails.

My family moved again after junior high and I lost track of Luther. I was in a bigger high school and had new interest, but I never found that one guy like Luther again, until my junior year. Luther showed up my third year with an automobile and we picked up where we left off. We double dated and ran around together as much as possible. We were even given the job of filling the candy machines in the hall ways our junior year and had that hour together. By this time my brother Aaron had other interest so I once again had a true buddy.

True Buddies forgive each other. I had a new girlfriend and she was the only thing that came between him and me, but he had girlfriends too. In fact, he was sweet on one of my girlfriend's friend, but had not been able to get her interested. One night there was a slumber party at her house and my girlfriend was there. Like two young American boys we thought we'd hang out in the neighborhood. They soon discovered we were circling the house and before we knew it the police descended on us. We begged and pleaded ourselves out of that one. I told Luther it wasn't a good idea after the first ten minutes or so, but he was trying to get Linda's attention, and he did. Of course I was mad at my sweetheart too but she convinced me it wasn't her idea to call the cops on us.

Along with brother Aaron, we were planning on joining the service together. That didn't work out and he and Aaron went the Navy route which I thought was a lousy idea. Have you ever seen what those guys wore in boot camp? He credits my big brother with pulling him through those trials and has always admired him. We remained in touch and I stood up for him when he got married two years after high school but time and distance has kept us a part, but we stay in touch. We get together and visit now and then. I'll always be thankful that I had a good buddy to share my teens.

MOMMA'S YEARS

Ruby Sophia McGrew was born April 20, 1900 in Clark County, Illinois, the daughter of Charles Monroe McGrew, a lay Baptist Preacher, and Amanda Lathrop, a descendant of Joseph Lathrop who came over from England in the early 1600's. He too was a man of the cloth. Ruby would never know her father as he died December 30 in the year she was born. She had an older brother Jesse born in 1895 and two sisters, Edna and Goldie born in 1892 and 1898 respectively.

Her mother Amanda remarried a Robert Cunningham and had four more children. It is unclear what year Robert relocated the family to Arkansas, but Ruby grew up in Melbourne, Arkansas. Edna was married at age 16 and it is doubtful that she ever lived in Arkansas. Goldie made the move and met and married Ben Marchant at an early age, prior to her mother dying in 1915. My mother inherited the task of helping to raise her younger siblings until she was old enough to embark on her own by moving in with her sister Edna and her husband. For whatever reason, she was never again close to the Cunningham family.

She was independent and twenty years old working in a shoe factory in Charleston, Illinois in 1920 when she met a tall dark good looking farm boy from rural Coles County. No one knows how long the courting lasted, but on September 24, 1921 they were married and started a life together for the next thirty one years. It was difficult years being the wife of a farm hand and construction worker with an ever growing family, but she was very content having turned her life over to Jesus and trusting in him every day of her life. The only thing that she ever demanded in life from her family was that they not only get her to Church on time, but that they go along with her.

I don't know where the old upright used piano came from, but she soon learned how to play it and rejoiced often in praise on it, in the home and in Church Services. In some of the hard times there was no piano, but just as soon as possible Dad would see that she got another one. By age 40 she was a mainstay in the church playing the piano every Sunday Morning, Sunday Evening, and Wednesday Night. She could read a little music, but mainly she played by ear, and she knew hundreds of hymns. She and my Dad would often play and sing together. She had an alto voice and Dad was a lead singer and they shared that in the Church and other gatherings over the years.

If I've heard it once, I've heard the comment a thousand times about how wonderful a cook my mother was. She could fry chicken and bake bread, rolls, and pies that were out of this world, and her family was blessed. She worked with her daughters and they too developed into great cooks, but none ever ventured to say that they were as good as their mother. I truly don't remember store bought bread before I was thirteen years old. Homemade bread, still warm, with real butter would often greet us children when we came in at the end of the day.

She wanted to stay longer, but prayed to God thy will be done. Life had just gotten a little easier for her when her health failed her. She had difficulties with her last pregnancy in 1937, but she stayed the course for another fifteen years before she died on Thanksgiving morning of 1952 in her home on Connelly Street in Paris, Illinois. For services and burial she was taken back to Oakland where she and her husband had lived for over twenty years, to the Pentecostal Church that she belonged to for so many years, although it had been moved. Two of her favorite Pastors did the service, and her burial was in the Oakland Cemetery. The snow had started falling the morning she died and had continued until the roads were snow packed and treacherous, but it stopped before the hearse got to the burial site. Brother Hayes, one of the Pastors told my Dad that she was ready to go home, but her only fear was that maybe the Lord would think she loved her husband more than him. My Dad wept when he told me that and said he wished he could believe that was true. He was to join her in her place of burial in 1983, but he knew she had found a better place long before then.

SIBLINGS, I HAD A FEW

The beauty of being the youngest of eight is you had a lot of people to look up to. My oldest brother was 14 years my senior and for my youngest years he just assumed the position of second parent, and I took it. To me he was an authority figure. As a kid he tried that with his next two younger siblings and got told where he could go. If he didn't get his way he'd threaten to jump down the well. This disturbed one of my sisters greatly, but the other just told him to go ahead. This kind of leveled the playing field.

Of eight children, someone has to be the middle child or children. It's a fact of life. By the time the 4th. child came along my parents had to be exhausted at trying to raise a large brood and the 4th. and 5th. kids got less attention and direction. You could say the older kids could help with the younger kids and make Mom's job easier, and it happened, but that didn't apply to those closer to their own age. When my 4th. sibling, a girl, was eight her older siblings were 10,12, and 14. They couldn't control an 8 year old, and so it went. That is why the middle kids, a boy and a girl were loose cannons.

It just so happened that this pair, being so close in age, had a spark for life that surpassed some of the others. They grew up fearless and naturally resisted authority. They bonded together and held off all attackers. While some of the older siblings were inclined to mother or father the last three children, all boys, the middle children said the heck with them, let them fend as we did, the little sissies. The played together and stayed together for most of their lives. When they married they were closest and their spouses accepted the fact that these two were best of pals and they visited often. But, I get ahead of myself. Getting back to the years when they were about 8 and 10. They were ornery.

Dale, the boy, had an inclination to build fires. When Mom wasn't looking he would sometimes sneak a few of the matches from the shelf near the stove. Edna, the sister, didn't seem to care and let him have his fun. He'd use them like candles and let them burn down to his fingers. This was all fine and dandy until they went to the woods one day down below the house in a deep holler by the stream. There was plenty of dry kindling so Dale made a little heap and set it ablaze. I expect it was a nice little bonfire until the window took it and found other fuel for it. It quickly got out of control and Edna headed up the hill to find help to extinguish it. More help was called in and the woods were saved, but not before it had been thinned considerably. For that, Dale lost all of his match privileges under serious threat, which he understood.

Although both dropped out of school early, they went on to successful lives with wonderful families of their own. The brother even had time to take this younger brother in so he could finish high school. His advice to me was too tough it out. I didn't get a lot of sympathy from him, but he and his wife gave my wife and I a lot of love. I loved to visit Edna and get her cheerful outlook on life. She worked hard all of her life and had no times for my woes, but I'll always think she most resembled by Dad in many ways. Both siblings were pretty no nonsense with their own kids, but they were also a lot of fun and were dearly loved. They were active and had a lot of skills until the very end. Unfortunately they left this life in 2012 and 2014, Edna going first.

The woods burning incident came up in conversation a few years ago at a family get together with all of us there. They didn't deny the old family story, but neither were they apologetic. In fact, Dale mentioned that he had driven down to the old home place not too long ago and concluded that the woods looked like it needed thinned out again.....

TALE OF THREE SISTERS

Eula, Hazel, and Edna, three names that were rather uncommon in the twentieth century. These are three sisters that were raised very much alike, but did not resemble one another or have the same personalities. Born in nineteen twenty four, twenty six, and twenty eight, they were the 2nd. 3rd. and 4th. children of Ruby and Adren Swinford. To them fell the task of helping their mother with four younger brothers while their older brother worked with his dad to help provide food and shelter for the family. They all lived through the worse depression in our American history. They knew the life of homemade clothes, pass down clothes and shoes, and homes that could get awfully cold on a long winters night. They knew what it was like to wait for the county dole of flour and fruit and gravy made with water for lack of milk. It was work instead of getting a high school education and early marriages looking for a better life than they could have at home.

Eula married at seventeen, was named after a friend of her mother from Arkansas, the sister of Ben Marchant who married Ruby's sister Goldie. Hazel married at sixteen, was named after a family friend Hazel Hunt. Edna married at nineteen, was named for Ruby's older sister Edna. Eula and Hazel saw their husbands off to war and were left with baby daughters to care for while they were in the service. Eula's husband did not come back, being killed in Italy in the spring of 1945, but Hazel's husband survived the war in Europe. Edna met and married her husband, an ex-marine in 1947. He had served in the south pacific. Eula was to remarry in 1947 and had a son. Hazel had seven children in all, five living to maturity and Edna had a total of six children.

The sisters all were very close to their mother until her death in 1952. The girls themselves had a rather unique relationship with one another. It will always be a mystery of why this was, but it was undeniable. Eula and Hazel were very close. Eula and Edna were very close, but Hazel and Edna got along best when Eula was present to keep the peace. I had a battling relationship with the brother next to me in age as a child, but when we matured we became very close. Why that didn't happen with the girls no one can say.

Eula was the smaller of the three, but more assertive and commanding. This is the way she operated at home and on the job all her life. Hazel was bigger boned and taller than the others who perhaps worked the hardest and longest of them all raising her family. Edna was the easiest going one of the three who could give and take with the best. She could be tough and she could be tender. Hazel and Edna lost their husbands relatively early in life during the middle eighties. Eula's husband died in the late nineties and all three spent several years on their own.

All three raised beautiful families with many accomplishments of their own. While they themselves had very little formal education, many of their children did strive through hard work to get as much education as they could. In all the girls and their brothers gave their parents thirty-two grandchildren, twenty-eight living to maturity. They were each the backbone of their families and were well loved by their children.

Unfortunately their time came to leave this earth all too soon for the rest of us. For two it was Alzheimer's with the third one lasting longer with complications hard to determine, but the result was about the same. Two died in 2009. Eula had just turned eighty five and Hazel was eighty-three. Edna died in 2013 just after her eighty fourth birthday.

Each brings beautiful memories to me. Memories of the tenderness and love of Eula, the encouragement and laughter of Hazel and the fun and games with Edna. It was a special time in my life when Edna took up golf and loved it as much as I. We didn't play together often, but it was very special to me. Eula lived so many years in the west but came back home in the early nineties. I'm so glad that she did and that we had those years to get reacquainted. For Hazel it always such an special time just to visit her and get some of her cooking, if I was lucky, because she just raised my spirits. The memory can bring a smile to my face any time. Thank you God for these three special ladies in my life.

THE CHARACTER OF A MAN

You can live many years without knowing a person, but then under certain circumstances the veil begins to lift. That's the way it sometimes can be between two brothers. It doesn't always reveal everything, but often it reveals the core of a person.

This is the way it was for two brothers separated in age by over six years. By the time the younger neared maturity, the older one was married and he and his wife were saddled with many trials. A lack of education for him caused a real hardship finding work in an economy that was struggling for everyone. Although he was an extremely hard worker, having worked since he was an early teenager, his lack of skills didn't open many doors for him. The following is one story that he shared with his brother a little later in life. A story that illustrates what a man will do when he has to, and what the limitations his character put on him.

He was at his wits end trying to provide for a wife and child and keep a roof over their head. He was out every day looking for work but was not having much success in finding anything but an occasional job for a day. Things were desperate when he heard about a selling job. This was the last thing he wanted to do, and really the thing he felt least equipped to do, but he needed work so he looked into it. He learned it was a door to door job selling insurance, but he would have to wear a suit and tie and he didn't have either.

After thinking it over, he remembered that he had a cousin that he was very close with that had a suit. His cousin was taller, but nothing was said about it having to fit perfectly. When he checked with him his cousin was happy to help him out. The back of the coat had a rather significant three corner tear, but his wife stitched it up until it was barely noticeable. He took the job and was given the sales pitch and a few tips on how to appeal to the person answering the door. He was told to report early for work at a given place and he would be transported to the area where the team would be working.

The man designated the team leader drove some distance to a small town and dropped each of the men on the sales team at a different location. He started them off on foot telling them he would be back at a given time to pick them up. With a supply of applications and a few dollars for making change from the team leader, he started down the block in what appeared to be an older run down section of town. His job was to sell a product that cost four dollars a month and get the first month's payment in advance.

There were a lot of houses that he didn't even get an answer to his knock. Then there were some that gave him a quick brush off or some who would politely listen and then say no, they couldn't afford the insurance. This went on all day as he went up one side and then back down the other side of the block, and then moved on to the next block. He was barked at by dogs and had doors slammed in his face but not once did he find a buyer.

It was late in the afternoon when he knocked on a little run down house at the end of one block. The door was answered by a tired looking young woman with kids hanging all over her, mostly in rags. He could see through the door that pickings were very slim there, but he had her attention so he made his pitch. He could tell that she was trying to listen with all the distractions caused by the kids, but it was clear that life was really tough for her. At the end of his spiel, she said she'd buy one and would have to go find four dollars. The brother stopped her in her tracks and said, you don't need this now. As bad as he needed the two dollars he would make from the sale, he couldn't let her do that. He thanked her and walked away. From there he went to the designated pickup place and waited. That was his first and last day on that job.

When he revealed that story to his brother, he was telling him a lot about his heart. Even if you are in misery, you don't take advantage of other's misery. His luck didn't change overnight, but he and his wife made it through. He finally found steady work at a major foundry forty miles north of where he lived. He was there when his younger brother needed a home to finish high school, and they took him in. He was there when his younger brother needed a vehicle to get to and from work after school. He put up the money. He was there to help his younger brother get a job in the foundry when he graduated from high school.

Oh, the older brother liked to put on a gruff exterior at times, and he would do this with his brother and others. He could tell it like it was, and sometimes it might bruise feelings, but often it helped. With all this he had a zest for living and he and his wife raised a beautiful family. When he left this world, he left behind many beautiful memories. He also left behind a brother who got to know him well, and learned the character of the man.

THE QUIET ONE

Among the loud, the boisterous, and the aggressive, you will often find a quiet one. Perhaps in a large family it may not seem good for him or her, but in the long run it may be a good thing. In our family it was James Cleo.

For a brief period my parents lived in town when Cleo was born in 1933. He was probably the only one not born in the country. Shortly thereafter though he was back in the country where he would stay until he was nine years old. He was a small child with curly hair and he took a lot of kidding about that from his brothers and others.

Early on he found a protectorate in an older sister who showed him a lot of preference and even managed to get him into school a year early. This resulted in him being among the smallest and youngest of his classmates, which probably contributed to his shyness and quietness. Even among his brothers, he would be the one who stood back and let the others take the lead. By the time he got to Paris in 1945 when he was twelve, Cleo had already attended four different schools. His fifth school was the high school and he did go out for football but because of his size he was at a disadvantage and he didn't pursue it. After three years his parents moved to another community and rather than start another new school where he didn't know anyone, he opted to drop out and find a full time job. At age 17, that was the beginning of a long period of steady employment for many years. By age 18 he was married and at age 19 he was drafted into the Army and had a son. He was to spend two years at Fort Sill Oklahoma instructing on the care and firing of giant howitzer cannons during the Korean War. From my discussions with him, it is my feeling that this was not the best of experiences in dealing with the trainees that he had to deal with. Again, his quiet demeanor and relatively small stature may have contributed to this.

As he grew older and had sons of his own, he began to come out of his shell more each year. He became more active in his church and learned to play stringed instruments and performing. This did not result in aggressiveness or becoming loud in a crowd, but it did build his confidence. He spent over 36 years working for the same employer and was an exemplary employee. He grew deeper and deeper into his faith would quietly talk about it with others. He developed many friendships and was a loyal and trusting friend and brother.

He was there for this brother several different times when he made a difference. He and his wife gave this newly wed their home for a weekend when they had no place else to go. This brother called on him to be his best man in his wedding when the brother who was going to do it could not show up. This brother gave me the needed transportation when I was in the army and had none. This brother looked after his older sisters when they were ailing and in nursing homes. He was the stalwart one in the family who put family first.

As he grew into adulthood he became Jim instead of Cleo that the family always called him. Along with the name change, he himself became the more confident man that attracted others to him. Always a hard worker, after retirement he didn't slow down very much. Losing his beloved wife Tilly in 1990 was a terrific blow, but fortunately he found Betty who helped restore him to where he was and they have become a terrific Christian team that have enjoyed so many good things together. They have so much in common when it comes to gardening, restoring homes, and even for a number of years they did a lot of golfing. Now in their senior years they winter in Florida where they again have established new friendships and activities that they enjoy. In the end result, the quiet man has become quite a man, well respected and loved by family and friends.

A SIGHT TO BEHOLD

The year was 1945 and there standing alone in our yard was a sight to behold. My brothers and I weren't allowed to approach it as the glow was perfection and was not to be messed with. It just wasn't worth the punch in the arm to risk getting too close.

Our brother Dale had brought it home. It wasn't new, but it was customized and beautiful. I will admit that I'm not sure of the name Dale gave it, but it had one. I'll just call it Black Beauty, because it was coal black. The metal work from the front to the rear had an enamel black glow about it. We had never seen anything quite like it.

On the front and rear wheels were fender skirts covering at least one half of the tire and the sparkling spokes. Fastened to the ends of the handle bar were flowing tails of some animal, most likely a squirrel, but it could have been fox. On the front fender was a light to show the way through the dark, and on the handle bars was a rear view mirror. This was unbelievable. Where did Dale get it? A King's ransom could not buy such a vehicle, but there it sat. It's true that Dale at fifteen had a real job, not just paper routes like some of us. I know our parents must have given him the third degree, but it remained.

Did this eight year old ever ride that bicycle? No way. I wasn't even allowed to touch or wash it. Dale kept that Black Beauty shined to the nth degree all day every day. He developed a precedent then that he always followed on any vehicle he ever had, whether it was old or new. He loved bicycles and automobiles and knew how to take them apart and put them back together again. Some of those skills were learned from his older brother who brought much of that knowledge back from his years in the military where he had maintained a motor pool for an Air Force strip somewhere in the Marianas. (South Pacific to the uneducated).

The day came when Black Beauty disappeared. Whether it was for a lack of funds or the fact that Dale hit the road to find work, I don't know. I'm sure he found a good home for it but not before he helped Dad secure a bicycle for the three younger boys.

It was about 1946 and Dad must have been working pretty steady because he and Mom decided the brothers and I should have a bicycle. Not just any bike but a brand new one. One evening when Montgomery Ward stayed open, Dad took Dale downtown to find a suitable bicycle. Whether he thought

Dale had a superior knowledge or whether he just needed him to ride it home is the unanswered question. Anyway, Dale or someone picked out what appeared to be the classiest Ward bicycle available. Dale rode it home through the dark streets and there it was on the porch the next morning.

In the sunlight it was a thing of beauty to us. It was blue, my favorite color, and had a streamline design. It wasn't a Schwinn or a Roadmaster, which were the cream of the crop then, but it looked super to us. We each got to take turns riding it. It rode swell to me. The older brothers seem to have some hesitancy about it but I thought they were crazy. Only after they got Dad involved was it decided that the frame was bent. Not a lot, but some. Dad talked to Dale and learned that he had jumped many curbs on his way home the night before. It was decided then that Montgomery Ward was not going to help us out. Needless to say, we never let Dale get close to our bicycle again. Like he ever wanted to. We rode the wheels off of that bicycle over the next four or five years, even though we always made two tracks in the snow.

The question on my mind today is, does Black Beauty adorn someone's collection now and be worth thousands of dollars? Did some Picker dig it out of a trash heap? I'll never forget the way my brother loved that one of a kind two wheeler and the way he looked riding it full steam down the street. He must have felt like the Lone Ranger. And also, I might be able to remember Black Beauty's real name if I had gotten to ride it just one time.

CHERRY PICKER

I just recently had a birthday. They seem to come around faster anymore. Anyway, per usual my wife asked me what I wanted for my special day. As always I had no clue. I could have asked for a new car, but the old one is barely broken in. I could have asked for the moon but I know I wouldn't get it. So after some deep thought I told her what I really wanted, a cherry pie.

One of the reasons I married this woman is for the crust she makes for pies. When she kneads that dough and puts all that love into her labor, people who have shared it with me sincerely acknowledge just that. She makes a great pie. For years the kids and I have always looked forward to them. I could have asked for an Angel Food Cake which is great too, but this day I opted for the wonderful crust versus the wonderful icing.

Now I normally am not selfish and I preach that giving is better than receiving, but when it comes to her cherry pie I am sorely tested. It seems that my kids wanted to come over and celebrate the day with me. I asked if the pie would be enough and she explained only three of the family could come. I pictured the sections of the pie being cut and resigned myself to the fact. You see, I love my kids too. True to form, the pie was delicious.

I've always had a love affair with cherries. I first fell in love on O'Kalla Street in Paris, Illinois where we had not one, but two cherry trees in our backyard. Each year I couldn't wait for them to ripen. Each year I grew a little taller so I could reach more lower branches from the ground as I knew Mom didn't like us climbing in the tree. When they ripened she had us pick those cherries for pies and canning. I always tried to put at least two out of three in the bucket. The birds took care of the seeds on the ground before she saw them. We used ladders so as not to break down limbs.

Then it happened. In 1946 my brother Owen came home from the Army. After two years on a South Sea island he returned to us. He opted to have his own living quarters, but he was at home a lot working on cars in the side yard and just being with family. One day the brothers and I were sneaking a few cherries and he told Mom and got us scolded. "Don't you boys want any left for pies". We didn't like to be scolded by our mother. The next step after scolding was a switching off the old willow tree standing in the yard. Owen squealed on us and we were not happy.

A day or two later who did we find sitting up in the fork of one of the trees but our big brother. I couldn't move fast enough to go and tell my mother on him. She came out and he sat there eating cherries. He said, "Mom, I'm just cleaning my teeth" and went on eating. Mom just smiled and gave him a pass. I guess the fact that he was home after being away for over three years gave him a right to eat cherries and have cherry pie too. I don't even recall him helping to pick the cherries later either.

Even today when I'm driving through the country I watch for cherry trees. They are so rare. I don't know where cherries come from anymore. My wife and I lived in the country with our kids, cats, and dogs for ten years. I ever planted a dwarf cherry tree. I think the birds allowed me a harvest of 8 or 10 cherries a year, hardly enough for a pie. So today we buy store bought canned cherries for our pies. With her touch she brings me joy and memories of those delicious pies that my mother made years ago with cherries picked with my own boyish hands.

A MAJOR SUCCESS STORY

My Dad would say, 'none of my five boys ever ended up in the Penitentiary'. Under the conditions they were raised, maybe that was an accomplishment. He also had three daughters who did not shame him but maybe that wasn't quite as important. Now to be open and truthful about this whole character thing, he did have some help. Her name was Ruby. I'm sure the siblings were as conscious as I that we didn't want to do anything to hurt our mother or make her ashamed of us. We would always have her unconditional love, but we didn't want to see anything in her and dad's eyes but love and pride.

Our folks didn't have anything but a very basic education. Neither of them got past the eighth grade, if that far. They didn't overly stress schooling to their children, but they did work to teach them common sense and do the things they needed to do to get by. With times so difficult in the thirties, schooling was put on the back burner and consequently none of the first six children ever finished high school and some didn't get more than an eighth grade education.

All of the girls were married before they were twenty, one of them marrying at sixteen. They did just fine with good husbands resulting in good families. One was widowed by the war and left with a daughter. She remarried and had a son. One's husband served in the Army in France and they subsequently had seven children, and the other's husband was a Marine in the South Sea Islands and they had five children.

There was a eight year gap in age from the first son to the second but their working lives took similar turns. The oldest in the middle thirties was working at age of 13 or 14 to help farm and whatever it took to help the family survive in the 1930's. The second son was doing men's work and trying to be independent in the war years at age 14. The war had disrupted everyone's lives. The younger three had less tumultuous lives coming of age after the war. All three served in the military. Dad was proud of all.

In my mind though, one stands out. He was the one who probably had less direction as a middle child and ended up growing up too fast. In 1944 he was living on his own and working for a living. At age 16 he was working in an auto plant in Chicago as an adult. At age 17 he was working the wheat fields of Kansas to make a living. At 19 he was married with a son. He was the hardest worker of all, but he also lived the hardest of all. By the age of 23 he was working in a General Motors Foundry doing the dirtiest and greasiest jobs. He was thrown in with some of the roughest crowds and held his own.

By age twenty-six he had taken his family to Texas to try and improve their lot. He did everything he could to make it, but at age twenty-nine he was back in Illinois, down on his luck with a sick family. A young man getting old very fast.

Along the way he had picked up skills and was developing as a carpenter. He took it seriously and learned all he could from his dad and others. He got a break and went to work for a reasonably large construction firm in Champaign, Illinois at the bottom level. Over the next twenty years he self-taught himself the building trade, and by the time he had been in the business ten or twelve years he became the head superintendent for the firm running major jobs building commercial buildings and schools. With an eighth grade education he had mastered the art of blueprints, layouts and surveying. People who had known him earlier in life marveled at what he had accomplished.

Dad didn't live to see everything that Dale had done in life, but he saw enough to know that his middle child with probably the most difficult start in life had made him proud, and the rest of us too.

1939 PLYMOUTH COUPE

He had never had a four wheel vehicle before, and he wanted one. His senior year in high school he dropped out of all organized sports and went to work across the street from the high school at Toby's Shell Station. He still played some intermural basketball, and in my opinion his team could have beat the high school varsity team that year. Most of the guys were ones that couldn't along with the high school coach. Before long though, he was doing all the things that a service station did such as oil changes and greasing cars because he had a knack and love for messing around autos. He had learned a lot from being a gofer for his big brother who had been a motor pool sergeant in the Army. Many a vehicle had seen repaired in our side yard at our home on O'Kalla Street. Aaron was a thrifty guy, you'll note I didn't say tight, and sure enough the day came when he had saved enough for a car. He only needed about a hundred dollars back them.

Our brother Dale was looking for a chance to change cars. His family had gotten bigger and he really needed more than the two passenger car that he had. He made a deal with my brother Aaron and sold him his light grey two seated 1939 Plymouth Coupe, complete with radio. It was exactly what Aaron wanted. He now had his very own automobile. He had had motor bikes and lots of bicycles, but never a car.

This was in the fall of 1952 and our mother had just passed away at Thanksgiving time. We were still living on Connelly Street but dad was looking to move somewhere else as the memories were just too much for him. Aaron and I were old enough to look after ourselves being almost eighteen and sixteen respectively, so our dad went where the work was to make a living for us. Construction work in the Chicago area was the most promising and he ended up in a suburb of Chicago where he would work all week and then come home on a Friday evening. Then he would get up early on a Monday morning and make the trip back to Chicago. He roomed quite often with an older Swedish couple that had a spare room for rent. I don't know the number of times that Dad told the story about these sweet people who were immigrants and still spoke with heavy dialects. He often dined with them and the older gentlemen would complain to Dad about his favorite part of breakfast. He said, "they used to call it yelly, yelly, and now they call it yam" with Dad adding the accent. In the meantime Aaron and I attended school and fixed our own meals. We always knew we could get a hot meal downtown at Bill's Café and have him put it on the tab and dad would pay him later. We never lacked for anything except his presence. That was tough enough.

Aaron's car was serving his purpose very well and he had an active dating life and was doing well in school. His car, however, had just one major flaw. I don't fully understand what the product was in 1952, but his radiator would not hold an anti-freeze, it would all boil out. The only solution was to make sure the water would never freeze in the radiator. When the cold weather hit, any time the car would be sitting for an extended period of time the radiator would have to be drained. This is what had to be done for every freezing night. Sometimes I'd help him. It was no big job. Refilling it was the tougher chore because there were no outside faucets or hoses. As long as the water was not allowed to freeze in the radiator, everything would be okay.

One freezing Monday morning dad had taken off at four o'clock to make his Chicago starting time. Aaron would always be awake and see him off and then come back to bed. That particular morning dad had just left when Aaron came in and shook me awake and said we'd have to catch up with dad, he'd left his overcoat behind and would need it. We jumped into the 1939 Grey Plymouth Coupe and started our chase up Route 1 toward Chicago. I'm sure Aaron was gaining on my dad who was not a fast driver, when after about five miles the chase was over. We had forgotten to refill the radiator and dad had to do without his coat that week.

The motor was ruined in Aaron's first car, but with the help of our brother a used engine was found and Aaron was back in business again before the month was over. The replacement engine probably cost as much as the car did originally, but he did what he had to do. We later moved to the country and I would depend on him for transportation many times as dad was still working up north. He drove that old grey Plymouth until late 1954 when the new cars came out. We just happened to have a brother selling Plymouth automobiles and Aaron ended up with a brand new 1955 Cherry red Plymouth with twin chrome tail pipes that he could make drag the payment on a fast take over. That was his second automobile. A lot flashier than the old grey Plymouth, but not more loved. I remember both of his first autos very well. He even let me drive them.

A GOLD STAR

According to one source, the Encyclopedia Wikipedia, there were 60 to 65 million deaths during World War II of men, women, and children around the world. This tragic period officially extended for six years and one day from September 1939 to 1945. The United States declared war after Pearl Harbor on December 7, 1941 and continued until the surrender of Japan on August 19, 1945.

This period changed the world. No country or family was left untouched in some way. For one thing, communications to the Almighty was undoubtedly tremendously increased. I doubt there were few households that had family involved in the U.S. that didn't fill the air waves with prayers daily. My home surely believed in prayer. I grew up singing about the "Royal Telephone", just one of the many hymns about talking to God. It started, 'centrals never busy, always on the line. You can talk to Jesus almost any time'. My mother was a prayer warrior, a description that wasn't commonly used until later years.

In 1943, three of our family was in the service. My older sister's husband Louis Childress, my second sister's husband Marvin Duzan, and my older brother Owen were all in the Army. In 1945 Louie was in Italy, Marvin in France, and Owen on Guam in the South Pacific. This trio kept the messages to heaven going strong everyday by my mother and others.

Someone came up with the idea of hanging a small banner in the window in homes that had family in the service. Mom wasn't one to normally follow trends, but this one she was in for, hook line and sinker. Our home had one with three blue stars proudly showing. It was an idea that really caught on and hundreds of thousands of windows across the country were adorned with the banners. That banner stayed there until the end of the war except she had to replace it with a different one in April 1945 when Louis Childress died of wounds while in battle in Italy. One blue star was replaced with one gold star. The banner took on a more solemn meaning to all of us. Tragically Louie died just a month before Victory in Europe was declared. Thankfully the other two boys, now men, came home safely.

About three years later Louie's remains came home too. A ceremony was held in the little St. Elmo's Cemetery between Oakland and Ashmore, Illinois where his family has a plot. Present was his little daughter Donna who couldn't have had any memory of her Dad, but then she was about six years old.

Mom was there for her Gold Star. He will always be a Gold Star for his family.

Mom prayed hard for all of her kids and it must have helped because we too have kept the air ways open with our maker. Each of us has wanted to get his gold star.

MOMMY, WHY ARE YOU CRYING?

"My Daddy is only a picture, in a
frame that hangs on the wall,

Each day I talk to my Daddy, but he never talks at all.

I tell him all of my secrets, and all my little plans,

And from the way he smiles at me, I know he understands."

A song of the 1940's that pertains to many children that never got to know their Daddies. We know that hundreds of thousands of men and women were killed in WWII, and at the time Gold Stars shown in windows block after block in many cities and towns. From Pearl Harbor to VJ Day (Victory over Japan) there were many hearts broken and lives that can never be replaced.

It was March 1945 when the knock came on the door in Decatur, Illinois. The young mother's mother answered the door and a man wearing a western union uniform asked for the young mother, and then handed her the telegram.

Fearfully she tore it open and read the message from the Government. It said that her husband had been wounded in action in Italy and was in the hospital there. She would be kept appraised of his condition as it became available. Her mother and father comforted her and sat with her as she sobbed. Her little girl was asleep in the bedroom.

In early April 1945 there was another knock on the door. This time the young mother answered to find another western union delivery man. With trembling hands she accepted the message and slowly opened the envelope. She almost immediately went to her knees gasping and sobbing and her parents knew it was the news that they dreaded the most. Her husband had died of his wounds in Italy. This time her tiny daughter, now two and a half years old starting tugging at her momma's dress and asking her, "What's wrong mommy"? Her momma took her in her arms and for many hours and many days she would cry and sob, with the little blond daughter asking many times, "what's wrong mommy"?

It would be years before the little blond girl would truly understand the magnitude of the loss, but because she didn't have the memory of her father it was different. She and her mommy would continue to live with her grandparents until her mommy remarried when she was five. She had grandparents that adored her and uncles and aunts in the house that pampered her and loved her, but none could replace a father. Her Step-father loved her and raised her as his own, but all she truly knew of her father was what the family could tell her. When in 1948 his remains were brought back to the states and a ceremony was held for her hero father, she was there but at six it had to be confusing. All she saw was a casket.

Three other children, who were later connected to our family by marriage, had that same type loss. The older girls have a memory of their Daddy but the little boy did not. They basically were fatherless for all their youth until their mother remarried when they were in their teens. For them, all they had for years was the memories and the picture that hung on the wall.

Many years have come and gone, but today and tomorrow's generations need to be reminded of our heroes and the sacrifices families made. Many lives were affected when lives were lost.

"The Angels took Daddy to Heaven,
when I was just going on three,

I'll bet they never told him, how sad and lonely we'd be.

I try to cheer up my Mommy, when
the tears roll down her face,

My Daddy is only a picture, but I'm
trying to take his place."

Lyrics written by Thomas C. Dilbek

BIG BROTHER

Tag along. Kids probably thought that was my name because big brother was always saying that to me. I was like a shadow and he frankly got a little tired of it. My big brother, for parts of our lives, was a head taller than me and was one busy guy. He normally found something interesting to do and I didn't want to miss out.

It was probably in one of our disagreements when I was about five that I gave him his first longest lasting scar. I'm not sure why I had a tin can full of rocks just right for throwing, but throw them I did and it caught him just above the eye. Maybe it was an innocent game of combat or something, but nevertheless I marked him for life. He returned the favor not too long afterwards when he closed the car door on my finger distorting the nail and finger for the rest of my life. I recall specifically the reason for that one. He was pretend driving and I thought it was my turn.

It was in that same period that he got favoritism that I'll never forget. Just because he was sick, it could have been whooping cough, or measles, or mumps or one of those diseases, and my mother sent out and got him a professionally made milk shake. No one could explain to me how that could have been fair in any way. I was treated very badly.

As we grew up we fought a lot, and we fought together a lot. Fighting was a big thing in our elementary years in the school yards and the neighborhood. He would never hesitate to step in and have my back regardless. Mom always said we fought like cats and dogs, but she didn't always see us pairing up to take on others. This was all before the video games and such. My family had the standard that we never hit anyone in the head. Dad preached that and we didn't. The stomach, back, and arms were fair game. My big brother and I were competitive about everything, especially sports. By being so, we made each other better and it made a major difference in our lives.

My last two years of high school we grew very close. Often, we were all we had as Dad was working away from home a week at a time. We got up together, went to school or work together, and took our meals together. We even double dated together. We had planned on going into the service together but I got antsy and joined before he was ready, and also we ended up in different services. He liked the Navy. He was even one of the first to approve of the high school sweetheart I found and later married. We were to be each other's best man but that didn't work out.

After his Navy years he found a job with International Business Machines. They sent him to extensive schooling and he launched a twenty year career with them maintaining IBM computers in different parts of the United States. After twenty years he took early retirement and went into business with me in computer services for the small businessman, and also as a part of my C.P.A. practice. He had other interest also, in Chrysler Dealerships and other things. In the interim he went to a Junior College and got an associate's degree in Accounting and actually taught classes for that same college.

Our businesses separated in 1985 but we still worked together whenever we could. We knew we could call each other with questions or support and our families have always been close. I know that today I'm a better man because I had a big brother that I could look up to, and he has never failed me with his honesty, his loyalty, or his love. Thank you big brother, I would love to give you one more big punch in the arm. I think I owe you one.

DOUG'S STORY

From a great family with two older sisters and one older brother, Doug had the usual childhood growing up in Illinois. Rather small for his size, he was very popular with his cousins and friends and was looking to a very bright future. His mother was encouraging more education after high school, and his dad had an entry way into the same business he was in, but Doug chose to go his way.

He married his high school sweetheart, got active in a Protestant church even though he was raised Catholic by his mother, and even entertained the idea of becoming a Youth Minister. He had secured a job with a large power company when his daughters started being born. He would end up with three daughters in a period of five years.

In 1984 at the age of 24 he was diagnosed with Primary Scierosing Cholansitis of the Liver. The condition continued to deteriorate until a transplant had to be done in 1991. His health and pending future condition put a lot of pressure on the family but he continued to work as he could and provide for his family. It was before he had the transplant that his wife told him that she wanted a divorce. She would stay with him until the transplant was completed, but that she wanted to leave the marriage. As soon as he recovered, true to her word she left the home place, leaving the girls behind. In 1992 a divorce settlement gave them joint custody, but that they would continue to live with their dad. The girls were seven, five, and twenty-one months old. From that day he regained his strength and was able to work and provide for them until they were grown. He dedicated himself to that task. About ten years later he did get married again but with health issues and family issues it didn't work out. Doug's liver was failing him once again. It was a rare happening that anyone would qualify for a second liver, but he did in 2004.

Things did not always go smoothly, but through all this he maintained his job with the Power Company and all three of his girls went on to college. Two became nurses and one a financial administrator with very bright futures. It was when the youngest was about twenty years old that he met Lynne at a dance and they dated for several years before they married. Today Doug has a grandchild with the possibility of more to come. Two daughters are married to professional men and the youngest daughter works in the Mayo Clinic in Florida having gotten her advanced degree in nursing. Is there any wonder the family is proud of all of them, and especially of Doug who persevered through the most difficult of times?

NIECE, WHERE HAVE YOU BEEN?

The childless couple had waited twenty-eight years and never had a child. One day the man's mother mentioned that she had been talking to two ladies that worked at the Shoe Factory where she was a Supervisor. One of them had a sixteen year old daughter who was pregnant out of wedlock and looking to find a good home for her baby when it arrived. Of course the couple jumped at the chance to have a child of their own at last and a private adoption was set up. In July 1945 they had a new baby girl. They paid for the medical services and took the baby home with them.

The couple had a little land, but not enough to make a living. It was not an easy life but they did all they could to see that their daughter had what she needed in life. There was very little other family, basically just the grandparents and them. The baby grew to adulthood doing exceptional in school and won a scholarship to college where she got her teaching certificate and then went on and got her master's degree and proceeded to teach math for thirty-nine years in high school and junior colleges.

She married and had two daughters during her teaching career, but the marriage ended and after her parents died she had two daughters and two grandchildren, that was the extent of her biological family. Looking through her deceased parents papers one day she discovered her adoption papers naming her birth mother. She had always known that she was adopted but never was inclined to do anything about it while her parents lived, but now she started a search, to no avail. She ran into a dead end and gave up.

A few years later her daughter convinced her to try again as laws had changed and maybe things could happen. All she had was the birth mother's name and one day she found that family name in an obituary column. She noted that one of the sisters of the deceased had the same first name as her natural mother and she pursued that trail which almost immediately paid off. She not only found her mother, who unfortunately was suffering from Alzheimer's disease, but three half-sisters and a half-brother and they welcomed her with open arms.

They had not known and wanted to learn all the details of her life. Not only did her family expand immediately, it exploded as she learned she had over one-hundred and fifty direct relatives related to her natural mother. A dinner was held to welcome her to the family and she has made the effort to make it back each year for the extended family reunion, although she lives considerable distance away. It's been a wonderful reunion of family.

BRIAN'S STORY

A baby named Terry that became Brian James Swinford is a well-known story in our family. Having to be given up for adoption by a beautiful unwed mother, he came to the arms of Marilyn and Don that 23rd. day of July in 1965. He could not have made two people happier. He went through some awkward growing up years to become a man well loved by family and friends alike. At the age of thirty-nine he met the love of his life, Christina Phillips on November 6th. 2004. Brian has made a successful tax practice in Herrin, Illinois and both are deeply involved with their church. The beautiful story just improved when he re-discovered his birth mother and family and has grown very close with them also. A longer version of his life and pursuit of happiness is available for the asking.

COMING OF AGE

We've all done it. Life runs in stages. This topic may immediately take some of you to that age when you could get driver's license or be old enough to vote or drink, or taking on the responsibility of adulthood. All are legitimate stages of life. All are important. Are some more important than others, or more difficult?

You'll note one stage not mentioned above was that span from ages of 10 to 14. For many of us that was the coming of age and was the most difficult, the most bewildering, and the longest span to overcome. Think about it, did you just sail through those adolescent years with a constant smile on your face, or did you have crooked teeth, pimples, and awkwardness that put you into constant embarrassment. All of this and hormones. It's difficult to pin point which one is the more difficult. The question was whether we could live long enough to outgrow pimples, awkwardness, and the magnetic draw to the opposite sex. I'm sure both male and female had these trials, but I can only speak for me, a male.

It all started early with trying to impress the little girls, but it wasn't about sex, it was about popularity. There was no kissy stuff; it was all about laughter and skipping rope. You wanted to be the envy of your class with the cutest chick walking and talking with you. Playing ball and spelling bees had emotion, not girlfriends. These were the easy carefree days. Then things started happening in the body, in our growth pattern, and to our skin, especially on the nose. To my knowledge medical science has not found a way to prevent this stage or eliminate those white ugly puss filled pimples even today. They could come almost in a moment's notice when you were expecting them the least and someone would be sure and point them out with laughter. Of course you would return the recognition given the chance. It seemed that boys had more but I expect the girls were just better at covering them up. Maybe that is why makeup was invented.

I think it was the adults and not the kids that came up with the idea of Hayrides in the fall. The more advanced kids would pair off and cozy up in the straw while a lot of us would sit and look awkwardly at each other. A lot of those things were planned by the Churches. The hormones seemed to have a reverse effect on some of us. Where we had been the cock on the walk at age nine, we became the shy guys with the pimples. The transition was not easy. Some of those girls were wearing lipstick and other stuff on their faces. They had gone from ten to 16 overnight. They were the scariest. I almost was afraid to talk to them at school.

Then came the biggest test. My Mom made sure we were in Church two or three times a week. At least on one of those occasions, the little girls living across from the church would be there. They were Shirley and Nancy. Shirley was my brother Aaron's age and Nancy was my age. I don't recall which sister had a birthday, but my brother and I were invited and happy to go. We had cake, goodies, and games to look forward to. Of course brother Aaron was the draw because he was already nearing six foot tall and had beautiful well-groomed blond hair resembling some Nordic God. I would have given him a trim some night if I thought I could get away with it. I may have been an afterthought for the party, but I showed up anyway.

Things were going well and I was enjoying it when game time came along. Shirley, I'm pretty sure, explained the rules to the game of 'Post Office', no doubt a popular game for the under 15 crowd but a first for me. I think the rules were that two teams were made. One boys and one girls. The idea would be that the customer, the boys, would enter the post office where the postal clerks would send one of their numbers. A secret draw where the guy and girl would meet alone in a room for about 2 minutes and get acquainted without anyone watching. Seemed harmless enough to me. Although I already knew a number of the girls, it couldn't hurt to talk to them alone, and when I was called to get my mail, that turned out to be one quiet awkward two minutes. Dumb game.

The next game was a lot different. The idea was to form a circle and take turns spinning the bottle in the middle. If the bottle pointed to a girl, you were supposed to kiss her. Wow, where did that game come from? Didn't teach it in my Sunday School Class. If the bottle pointed to another guy, you would get a pass that time. To tell the truth, I think my luck ran out before the evening was over. Brother seemed to like both games just fine. Maybe that was why he was so popular.

Coming of age wasn't easy for me. I finally advanced to meeting a little girl in the local theatre on Saturday Matinees and holding hands. Of course she wasn't from my school. Even there I lacked skills. She was a twin and sometimes Kay and Rae would trade places which wasn't that easy to tell in a dim theatre. Bless their hearts. Didn't they know I already had enough problems? At least in that lighting they would have trouble spotting the zits.

LIVE AMMUNITION

I've never been a gun enthusiast. Whether that was because I never had the opportunity to hunt or because I had no desire to hunt is not clear to me. Dad had a shot gun, but I never fired it or wanted to. The only guns I ever truly wanted to fire as a kid were, first the 45 Automatic that my brother brought home from the Army. That was the automatic hand gun that he wore on his hip when he was overseas. I remember one outing in the country when the older guys all went out into the field and took turns shooting that gun and I wasn't allowed to. Too much kick for a kid, I was told. Secondly, my brother Dale had a 22 Rifle. It would shoot long rounds and short rounds. The long rounds were about 3/4ths of an inch long and traveled further. These rounds would have to hit something in a vital spot to be lethal, but they were good for shooting at cans. That was fun. That was my experience with guns and live ammunition before joining the Army.

Early on in basic training we were issued a weapon. The M1 Rifle weighed twelve pounds and would hold a clip of eight thirty caliber shells, I think. I believe that was called the Garand Rifle that became Army issue during WWII. Our first job was to memorize the serial number and keep it clean at all times. Our second job was to learn the different positions we were expected to hold it for marching and inspections. Our third job was to learn to take it apart and reassemble it as quickly as possible. Then we got to the business end. We then took it out on the bayonet course and learned how to kill with it in hand to hand combat. Fortunately our targets were all dummies and we'd lunge at them with the bayonet fixed on the end of our rifles and then withdraw. It wasn't until about the sixth week before we actually got to fire the weapon, but only after hours of drilling on how to do that also. Calibration of the site was very important for accuracy.

That week on the Rifle Range in the heat of the summer took its toll and most of it was waiting and watching before getting a turn to fire your weapon. Everything was done on white rock. You also had to take a turn marking targets. You were in the pits and would push the targets up over your head when others were shooting. At the cease fire you would pull the targets down and mark with colored patches the new holes in the target. When it became your turn finally, you'd load a clip of four shells and shoot at the targets from a standing and sitting position from three different distances. At the end of that week I was one sick guy, but that's another story. I didn't care if I ever shot another rifle.

Before we could complete basic though we still had two more challenges. I found the first one almost fun, but we only got one chance at hitting a junk tank on the hill side with a bazooka. But for some reason the Army chose to call them Rocket Launchers. In the comics and movies they called them Bazookas. This involved two guys. The loader and the firer. The firer would take his position kneeling on the ground and the loader would put one projectile in the rear of the Rocket Launcher. When the firer was tapped on the head he would then aim and try and hit the target. The loader had to be sure and stay clear of the rear of the weapon as there was a serious back blast. This was a very real experience, but the shell was always a dud. If you hit the target it would only bounce off of it. That was okay by me. I don't remember if I hit the target or not.

The second challenge was the more serious of the two. We had to toss a live grenade. This involved a bunker with sand bags on three sides about four feet high and open on the rear. We were carefully trained on how to hold the grenade, how to pull the safety pen, and how to launch the weapon at the target after holding it for a brief time. It was not good to launch it too soon and give the enemy time to return it to you before it detonated. It the front corner of the bunker was a round hole for emergencies. Grenades would get dropped accidently, guys could panic, and sometimes they would duck too soon and the grenade would not clear the four foot wall. In this case the grenade needed to be quickly pushed or kicked into this safety hole by the guy or the cadre at the rear of the bunker.

Often things in the army things were done alphabetically. For this reason I was in the back of the line that day and dreading my turn to have that kind of a weapon in the palm of my hand that could produce so much shrapnel. There were no instances of real trouble ahead of me, but every once in a while you'd hear someone getting chewed out for not following strict instructions. I was getting pretty close to my time when apparently they ran out of grenades and we were through for the day. I never got to throw a live grenade and I didn't care.

Thereafter each year we had to qualify on the range one time wherever we were, and in my last year we were taken to a Marine base somewhere in Virginia where we fired a thirty caliber machine gun. Of course the gun was locked into place and could not be moved left or right or up or down. It was aimed at a mound of dirt about thirty yards straight ahead. We'd squeeze off burst of six rounds a couple of times and my army days of live ammunition were over.

Since then I've fired at a pheasant or two with a 12 gauge shot gun that my Dad bought for me for helping him roof a house, but I didn't hit anything. I didn't let him know when I sold that gun to a friend a couple of years later. If my kids have ever fired a weapon, it wasn't when I was around. If I were threatened, I'd know how to use a weapon, but I wouldn't want to. You won't find any guns or ammunition in my home, but that's my choice.

COOL WATER

Everyone can look back over their lives and remember one or more times when they thought they would die of thirst. Three or four come to my mind immediately, and I'll never forget the experiences. 'Cool Water', the song, was the first solo I did in high school too, but that's another story. This is about thirst.

My most memorable thirst was in early August 1955. This stands out the most because it wasn't just me; it was a lot of fellow G.I.s put in the same boat. It started on a very warm day when I was pulling K.P. Kitchen Police (or army slavery) started before reveille and there were breaks only for meals. After the evening meal was finished, it normally took to about ten p.m. before the K.P's work was done.

Our company was on bivouac and camping out in a dense wooded area on the post at Ft. Leonardwood in Missouri. We had pitched our tents the night before and the K.P.'s were called on early to help get the food ready for breakfast. Being on K.P. was one time we could travel and dress lightly as it was too hot to wear full uniforms and we normally operated in boots, fatigue pants, and T-shirts. The wake up crew knew where we were by the towels we hung on our two man tents. Finding our way to the mess tent was a chore, but there were some lights.

It was a grueling day as K.P. always was. In fact, cooking and cleaning in the open with portable equipment made it more difficult. We did the best we could and by quitting time, we were exhausted. In the vicinity of the mess tents were the canvas water bags for the whole company. The troops were told to be sure and fill their canteens before turning in as the water would not be available in the morning and we would be moving out after chow. The guys not on K.P. still had their daily uniform on complete with canteens. It was no big chore for them to fill up before returning to their tents after dinner while it was still light. For the K.P.s, this meant that we had to find our tent in the dark after ten o'clock at night, get our canteen and find our way back to the clearing to fill up. We would then once again struggle to find our tent among the trees. I was so tired by the time I found my tent the first time; I decided to take my chances in the morning.

True to their word, the remaining water in the canvas bags had been dumped before revelry the next morning. We got our coffee, milk, or juice, but there was no water except for what was in our canteens. I wasn't the only one to make an unwise decision. By noon on that August day, the temperature had easily risen to 100 Degrees. By that time we had marched, attended classes, and did several things and many of us were out of water. We were heading in the right direction for fresh water, but we weren't getting there soon enough. Men started dropping out like flies and they had to sit us down in the shade and lecture us about our unwise choices. Some of the guys were passing out and someone finally figured that they had better make a special water run or face some serious consequences. I didn't pass out, but I wasn't walking either.

They had trouble getting the special water run and you could feel some panic among the cadre. The company commander, and he was a good guy, was making the rounds and checking on the guys that were down, including me. When the water finally arrived, it came with enough trucks to haul the whole company back to our barracks where we were dismissed for the rest of the day and allowed to shower and recuperate. I don't know how many were actually hospitalized from the incident, but it happened. I think someone might have reconsidered the wisdom of dumping water bags before breakfast again, even if it was warm water, and even if the troops were warned.

HALF A BUCK

I've never been a hunter, but that doesn't mean I don't know a bargain when I see one. Let me tell you about a bargain that I got involved with years ago. The year was 1955 and I was stationed at Fort Devens, which is located at Ayer, Massachusetts just thirty five miles outside of Boston in a rural area. This was the training post for the Army Security Agency, a service that a representative had talked me into.

When I joined the army I was given a choice because of my three year enlistment. The recruiter Sergeant in Paris, Illinois thought I was fit and would enjoy the Combat Engineers and I took him up on it. It sounded pretty interesting to be building roads and bridges for the infantry to cross in battling the enemy. At that time movies such as "A Bridge Too Far" had not been made by Hollywood or I would have run from him.

One of the first things the Army does is test you for aptitude etc. After a series of these tests, a recruiter invited me to join the elite Agency of Top Secret men for which I would have to have a background check by the F.B.I. Cloak and dagger is what it meant to this eighteen year old. I knew I'd pass the test because I didn't even smoke. This meant after basic training I'd trade my rifle for a top secret clearance and school at an exclusive post. Well the rifle came back later but it was a smaller one, and that is how I ended up at Fort Devens.

I'm not absolutely sure of what the Army was paying me in 1955 to go through the hell that was basic training, but it would never be enough. I didn't know human beings treated other humans the way those cadre treated us. Justification? They just wanted to save our lives. My folks disciplined me also for my own good, but they sure didn't use some of the army tactics. The brass didn't always know what went on down at the bottom of the pecking order. Anyway, I think we got about $65.00 a month and keep. That meant three meals a day, albeit some of them were WWII K-Rations, and a living quarters with forty-eight other guys, plus we had free health care, a clothing allowance, and free haircuts. After only four months in the Army, if we succeeded in getting through basic, we moved from an E-1 rating to a E-2 rating and got an eight dollar raise, but no more free haircuts. We were still privates.

After a two week leave at home following basic, it was off to Ft. Devens where army housing looked very much like the barracks in basic training. Thankfully though, treatment by the non-coms (corporals and sergeants) was better as long as we behaved and stayed shaped up. We'd have frequent inspections in the barracks and in the company area where we fell in to march to and from school each day. It was about a mile walk so we learned new songs to sing on the way led by a non-com. Some of them weren't songs our mothers taught us. We'd sit in various classrooms all day and then return to the company area for the evening meal. We did do sentry duty in the company area every couple of weeks. Life was pretty soft, but we were still in the army. One thing they would not tolerate was hair on the face or growing down on the neck. That meant haircuts at least every two weeks, or more often, at our expense.

One of the guys in the barracks that I had gotten to know was Carl Stephens from Idaho. I wasn't aware then that Idaho was known for growing potatoes, but in hind sight I'd say Carl might have been a potato farmer's son. He had a long drawn out western drawl, but it wasn't cowboy like John Wayne. He definitely was not city wise, so he just might have been a potato grower. We never discussed that. Carl and I put our heads together one day and came up with an idea that only two Top Secret intelligence guys could do. We decided to go down to the PX (short for Postal Exchange where you could mail letters, trade for foreign currency, or buy almost anything at discounted prices) and buy an electric clipper that in my memory cost under five dollars. Carl and I had decided we could economize by cutting each other's hair and invested in our own clippers, fifty/fifty.

Perhaps his hair was longer than mine, but anyhow I cut Carl's hair first. I had told him of all the years that I had watched my dad cut my brother's hair and my own with hand clippers, and I felt it wasn't a big deal. I didn't mention to him that my dad had clipped of the top of my ear when I was very young and how it would always be flat across the top. He didn't need to know everything. Cutting hair was just common sense. Cut it slowly and keep it even and all would come out right.

Carl had blond hair of a flaxen type feel, however that feels. Kinda like straw. Very different than mine. My first run through his hair with the electric clipper resulted in a large chunk of hair falling off his head, leaving a big hole. I immediately then started trying to even it up and the chunks kept falling and I was unable to get anything even. The end result was disaster. He couldn't be seen in public with what I had done to him and I knew it. It would take someone with more skill than I to take care of it. He's probably end up with a burr. He wasn't happy, but was ready to cut mine anyway. I decided that I'd pass getting a haircut after all and in fairness gave him my part ownership in the clippers. When I really seriously thought about it, a half buck at the P.X. Barbershop didn't seem like too much.

A SECRET MISSION

There it sat surrounded by an 8 foot fence. It was U shaped and there was 15 feet between the fence and the metal structure except for the area where there was a walk up to the entrance. It was guarded 24 hours a day by an armed guard, who also was the doorman. With the proper credentials, he would push a button and give you access. Three times a day you would see a steady flow of men going in and out of this structure, the building was never empty.

I had the credentials. I was part of a group of men that was referred to as a Trick that worked together and lived together, except for the officers and non-commissioned officers who had separate quarters. Our Trick would work 8 hours a day for seven days and then take four days off. We would then go to a different shift and repeat the same schedule. After the routine was established, the midnight shift would turn out to be the favorite shift for most of the guys. It not only had the lightest workload, but it also gave us daylight to do things when the shift was over.

What did we do? Under the threat of penalty of fine and imprisonment or both, I cannot tell you. I can only tell you that when we entered that building, most of the guys would turn left and occupy one wing of the building. A much smaller group would turn right and go through another locked door into the other wing of the building. I always turned left and to this day I have no idea what was in that other wing where the guys turned right. Truthfully, with the nerds that went over there I didn't care. They just didn't seem like regular guys to me and appeared pasty white. They never talked and we never asked because we did not have the 'need to know'.

Our mission required the clearance of TOP SECRET – CRYPTO. If we had the 'need to know', we could learn many secrets. That is why the threat always hung over us that we must never be captured by the enemies. We were always told that in case of an insurgence of any kind, we would be taken out and then the women and children. I thought that a little drastic, but if they said so who was I to argue.

Our work area composed of an elevated platform at the front of the room with three small desks on it. The long portion of the wing had small cubby holed areas with a small desk, a large radio signal receiver with ear phones, a chair and a special typewriter on both sides of the aisle. If you watched the men at work you would see them either turning dials on the receiver with their head phones on, or see them busy typing on their typewriters with head phones on. The three desks at the head of the room were for the Sergeant and the officer of the trick along with one guy who had the only different job in the room. He worked in conjunction with all the other men doing things that could be very important. Every so often you would see the sergeant make the rounds and collect the typed data from the different positions and give it to the officer who would then take it down the hall to the other wing. That was our job. Send typed papers to the other wing.

After 15 months of duty doing this, I naturally wondered how I contributed to the safety of the world and most especially of my country. I and the other guys had literally spent hundreds of hours collecting coded morse code messages obviously planning the next world war, and for our efforts we avoided it in my three years in the army. Those coded messages held all the secrets of mankind, and we had typed them and passed them on for someone to break that code and save mankind. But, because it was Top Secret material, we could never be recognized or decorated for our efforts. That's the thanks we get and to think I've kept those secrets for almost sixty years for my country. Well, I'm human so they are out now. You now have all the secrets that I have from my army experience.

Yes, I was vetted by the F.B.I. over sixty years ago and earned the Top Secret Clearance. Yes, I kept those secrets for over sixty years. Not one loose lip that sank a solitary ship. With that record there is no reason that I shouldn't have been qualified to be on the 'need to know' list maintained by the State Department. Apparently everyone else is!

DOING MY DUTY

"I will walk my post in a military manner, keeping my eyes ...." After sixty years I'm unable to quote my first general order that all the army troops learned as a first priority in basic training in the fifties. Violation of these orders meant trouble. This particular order stands out because of an incidence in Korea, 1956.

Starting in basic training every G.I. could expect two things, K.P. (kitchen police) and guard duty. At sundown of each day guards would be posted at strategic places to secure the army compound safe from invaders. The reasoning at Fort Leonard, Missouri may have differed from the war time use, but the job had to be done. The First Sergeant would cause a list to be posted each week naming those that would pull guard duty at any given time. You were expected to show up for inspection at the end of regular training, on your appointed day, dressed in a military manner with your weapon. You were inspected and then you were posted normally for a 3 hour shift, twice per night. It could be a stationery spot or one that required you to march around or back and forth. The Officer of the Day and/or Sergeant of the Guard would check on you periodically and you were expected to challenge them and get the proper password from them before letting them advance. Of course you didn't have any ammunition to stop them.

This differed in Korea as you were given one round of ammunition for your rifle for guard duty. I heard of G.I.'s in my company getting into trouble for shooting at rats, but not me. My army post in Korea was set in a small valley about five miles from Seoul. It consisted of fewer than 150 personnel and covered an area equivalent to about 8 to 10 acres. We lived in Quonset Huts with tarpaulin ends, inside of an 8 foot high barbwire fence with concertina wire on the outside. On one side was a gravel road with a Korean Village on another side, and Rice Paddies on the two other sides. Our company Motor Pool was across the road, but all living quarters were within about a 5 acre area on one side of the road with one entrance gate guarded by Security Police.

The powers that be worked up an incentive for the troops pulling guard duty. We were interrogated on our general orders and chain of command and evaluated by the Officer of the Day on our appearance and 'spit shine' on our boots. Clean rifles were also a qualifier. The nightly cadre to guard our post was about 20 guys. Officers, Sergeants and the cooks didn't have to pull guard duty, so our name would come up at least once a week. The sharpest guy would be given the night off, unless someone got sick or they were needed in an emergency. It was worth the effort to be sharp.

I got my share of nights off, but this particular night the Officer of the Day picked one of my Quonset bunk mates. I think it was due to the fact that they were both from Maryland, but there was no appeal system. Anyway, my post was a fence at the far end of the compound that ran along the Korean Village perimeter. It was about 100 yards long. I was to keep constantly moving back and forth along the interior of that fence.

I learned later that the Sergeant and the Security Guards at the main entrance had been trying to nab some Korean Black Market guys the night before, buying and selling things through the fence to the G.I.'s. It happened, I know. Me and most of the guys that I bunked with bought what we called 'Choggy shoes' through the fence with American dollars and cigarettes. They sure beat the combat boots for off duty wear. Seemed harmless enough to us, but I did get caught once and got an Article 9 or 19, can't remember which. The punishment was raking rock in the compound for four hours. Well anyway, it was probably a bigger deal than just shoes. They caught a guy whom they thought was involved in big transactions and roughed him up quite a bit. Turned out he was a respected member of the Village and no proof on any ties to the black market.

It was the next evening that I was walking my post in a military manner when I noticed a considerable crowd of villagers were gathering at the fence closest to the Quonset housing the First Sergeant. It was only about 50 feet inside the fence. They were unhappy and were shouting words that I didn't understand. The First Sergeant noticed them also and quickly decided that I needed to walk my post outside the fence to keep them away from the fence. With my one round of ammunition I marched out the gate and took up my post outside the fence. They backed up to let me stand by the concertina wire between them and the Quonset, but they were going nowhere. I was beginning to wonder what was going to happen when the Officer of the Day arrived on the inside of the fence and asked me what I was doing. When I told him, he immediately told me to get back inside the fence, go to my bunk and he would handle it. I had the rest of the night off and rumor had it that the Sergeant had gotten an A…Chewing for putting me in harm's way. Fortunately I did not have to fire my gun. When you do that you have to clean it, oil it and get ready for the next time that you have to do your duty and walk your post in a military manner. Diamond Jim, as the first sergeant was called, was not a popular man with anyone. Years later I saw him at the time trials at the Indianapolis Speedway and could not bring myself to go down and say hello. He probably wouldn't have remembered me or the night he tried to get me killed.

R AND R

I am very proud to have served three years in the United States Army. Fortunately my stint was in peace time and my only claim is that I helped keep the peace. During that time I spent sixteen months outside of the United States. I spent almost a month on a boat in the Pacific and fifteen months in Korea and Japan. I was nineteen when I got to Korea so this was a drastic change being away for family for the first time in my life.

In Korea in 1953 a peace was declared between the north and south, and the separation of the countries was designated at the 38th. Parallel. Since then, sixty-two years, infantry of the United States along with the South Korea allies have faced off against the North Korean Army. In 1956, the infantry lived in pretty sorry conditions under the stress of the enemy a few hundred yards away. For these men a rotation was set up for them to get a break by going to Japan for Rest and Relaxation or Recuperation, depending who was talking about it, or R&R. This is something the Army got right.

I was part of the Army Security Agency which was a significant distance from the 38th. Parallel. Our living quarters were better and we were always told that in case of an invasion from the north, we'd be evacuated first and then women and children. They didn't want men with our high security clearance and materials falling into the hands of the enemy.

On the down side though, we were not eligible for R&R. Once we got to Korea we could expect to stay there until our time was up. With a few exceptions.

The Army Security Agency Posts, and there were three in Korea, were all part of the Eighth Army, but set up independently of the Main Post. In all there were about five hundred men in this Group, and that is what we were called, and each month a contest was held. Soldiers were selected to compete in a Soldier of the month contest within their post, and the winner would then be sent to the headquarters of the group where the three men would compete against each other in front of a cadre of officers and non-coms. The winner would get recognition with photos, a fifty dollar gift and a week in Tokyo.

In January of 1957, just before my twentieth birthday, I flew in a cargo airplane from Kimpo Air Base in Korea to an airport just outside of Tokyo. This was a large cargo plane with two decks like they could haul jeeps and other heavy equipment. It just so happened that I didn't have much company as the Army in Korea was just put on Red Alert because of a situation at the Suez Canal. All R&R's were canceled. Mine was different so I was still allowed to go. It was a little lonely making that flight, especially since my memory was fresh about the incident that had just happened the previous month. One of these same type cargo planes had crashed coming to Korea killing many soldiers.

MEDICINE THE ARMY WAY

Following a night of pain in my left temple, I went on sick call. This involved a truck ride down to the 8th. Army Headquarters to see a doctor. There were dozens of servicemen ahead of me and I sat and suffered in the waiting room for two hours to see a doctor. The pain had come on suddenly and the only relief I could find was to hold cool water in my mouth. The colder the better.

The young doctor that looked at me gave me something for my pain. After consultation with others he decided that I needed to be hospitalized so that a battery of tests could be run. For this I would have to be transported to the Army Hospital thirty miles south of Seoul. The hospital was just several one story army barracks joined together. The Ward that I was assigned to housed approximately sixteen guys. It didn't take long for me to realize that I was in the United Nations hospital ward.

By this time it was a Friday evening. Just like the professions all over the world, the army officers were preparing to take their weekend. This meant that I was given pain pills and very little else for the weekend. Even with sedation I was sitting up in my bed holding water in my mouth until sheer exhaustion got me. Although they did take blood for test and other things on the Saturday, there was no serious effort to treat my problem.

My hospital bed was between an Englishman and a soldier of the Turkish Army. I soon learned that in addition to some other G.I.s, my Ward contained Canadian, Australian, and one Katusi soldier. Katusi was the name given the South Korean soldiers. He was at the far end of the Ward so I never really got the opportunity to talk to him. I don't think he spoke any English.

The guy from Turkey was a powerfully built guy with a big smile, and absolutely no English. He could not have been over five foot two, but he seemed very agreeable with everyone and everything. He had a condition that did not allow him to get out of bed and everything had to be brought to him. When he went to see the doctors, he went bed and all. That changed one day when an officer from his company showed up for a visit. In an instant he was out of bed and bowing and kissing the hand of the officer who treated him very nicely. Later I heard from others that officers had the power of life and death over the enlisted men under them. I don't know if that is true or not.

In less than a day I was ready to send the Englishman back home or shoot him if that wasn't possible. He spoke with the cockney accent and talked loudly all the time. Very obnoxious. It wasn't just me that he offended but several others also. I tried to get my bed moved but with no luck. No one else wanted that position and I would just have to take my turn. Because of him, I was not about to tell anyone that I too was of the English heritage.

I think my favorite of all the United Nations soldiers was the Australian. He had such a relaxed way of speaking and told stories about his homeland and his heritage. He was also a very good listener. He left a very good impression and the thought that one day I'd like to visit that country. The Canadian was also a good ambassador for his country, but the down under soldier had a certain charisma about himself.

The most interesting one was an older G.I. associated with one of the undercover agencies like the C.I.A. or whatever a counterpart was back in 1956. He must have been about 35 years old or older, with red hair and spoke without ever glorifying what he was doing. He just made it interesting, and it was usually about what he had encountered in the years between the wars. He was a career soldier.

After a very painful weekend, Monday morning came around and the senior doctors were on the job once again. Apparently they could not find anything with my blood test and other tests taken over the weekend, so they told me they were scheduling me for a spinal tap. They explained to me what that involved. In the interim, some of the other patients filled me in with other information. They had heard of guys being paralyzed when the needle went in wrong or other lesser severe things, so by the time the procedure began, I was up tight. All I could do was take the fetal position and wait.

I felt pain and I had a sore back afterwards, but I could still move my legs. They kept me on pain killers that helped but did not always stop the pain in my left temple. I was still spending nights sitting up in my bed trying to keep ice water in my mouth until I'd finally fall to sleep from exhaustion. It was about 24 hours before the doctors called me in and said they had not found anything. They would just have to observe me for a while longer and see is anything changed. They did indicate that while I waited though, it was noted earlier that I had a broken filling and they had set it up with the dentist to take care of that.

On Tuesday afternoon I kept the dental appointment and noticed soon after that the pain had ceased. I reported this to the doctor but he said it was not related. I had a good night's rest without medication and reported to them the next morning that I was not having the same type of pain any more. They decided to release me then and sent me back to my company with the order that I could no longer do the job where I would have to wear a headset on my left ear, because the pain had nothing to do with the filling.

The pain never did return. The doctors were wrong and I got a better job which did not require the headset. Everything worked out. When I returned to the states I went back to my old job and finished out my army service wearing headsets. For a week I had the unique experience of being a part of the United Nations Hospital Squad of Korea where we worked in harmony for peace in the world. Except for the English man.

HOUSE BOYS

It's been a lot of years since anyone asked me how things were in Korea. I assume by now they have seen the movies of the hell hole that it really was with the quagmire, the snow, rain, and living in foxholes with lots of people trying to kill you. Well, that's not my story. When I arrived there it was peaceful and quiet. For my particular M.O.S., it was a walk in the park. I know it differed with the guys up on the line, but that isn't the life I lived.

Stateside we had to work all the time with marching, practicing shooting, inspections, kitchen police, cleaning, and guard duty. In Korea we pretty much eliminated all of the above except guard duty and added on a job sitting at a console with ear phones day after day. With a little donation from our monthly stipends, we got all the rest done. Most of it was under the control of the staff, but we had some input on our houseboys.

For our money we had paid kitchen help, laundries, hair-cuts, seamstress, and sanitation workers to take care of our ten hole outhouse. We also had guys to clean our quarters, our rifles, and our shoes. To call them boys isn't correct as the average age of the houseboy exceeded those of the enlisted men. The Officers and NCO's had some older ones, male and female. Joe was assigned to our Quonset when I got to Korea. I'm guessing he was just shy of twenty-five. There was one thing I noted about some Koreans, they either looked like Chinese or Japanese and others mixtures. Both countries had controlled Korea at one time or another. Joe looked very Japanese. Except for about three months he was my houseboy in Korea.

I don't know how many years Joe had been on the job in the 330th. Company, but by the time I arrived he understood our English pretty good. His talking was laborious, but we didn't have any trouble getting our message across to him. He was a very pleasant guy and we learned to trust him with our things. Not all Quonsets were as lucky in that regard. He did an excellent job keeping our place ship shape and was more than just a little helpful in my being successful in my inspections and ultimate honors received there. We got pretty attached and most of us included him in our news and conversations. I'll never forget when he offered to pick up a fancy cake for my birthday to share with my bunk mates in Seoul. I sliced that baby and of course had to have the first piece. Little did I know that the Korean idea of icing is pure lard. Ever had a mouthful of lard? Well, Joe tried.

We were so attached to Joe that we always talked of getting him to the U.S.A. for an education, but as dreams go, we didn't know how to get the job done, and we were on our way home ourselves all too soon. I hope Joe has had a good life. He made the time I spent in Korea easier. I can't give the same accolades to some of the laundry people though. I sometimes got back rags. What did all that service cost? The total was probably less than five dollars a month or about 5% of our paychecks. Well worth it.

MY BUDDIES SECRET

I don't remember when we started talking to each other on a regular basis. Maybe it was when we were both attending an Army School in Massachusetts, or when it came time to ship out in a made over World War II B-24 Bomber used to transport army personnel. The flight was from Boston to Seattle and there were about thirty personnel aboard. All had been in my class at Ft. Devens, Mass., and all wanted to celebrate having graduated and console ourselves that we had just started our last week state side for the next sixteen months. George had not been in my barracks but during the flight we sat together for a part of the trip.

In Japan we regrouped and some of us were sent to Korea. That is where I crossed paths with George again. At the A.S.A. Headquarters south of Seoul, five or six of us were loaded into a deuce and a half truck and transported through Seoul to our assigned post at the 330th. A.S.A. Company about 5 miles north of Seoul. The A.S.A. stood for the Army Security Agency. Sitting in the back of that truck I noticed George had the biggest feet I had ever seen. At the company we were both assigned to the same Quonset hut and settled in. We were to work together for the next fifteen months. Working together also meant living together.

George was pretty pleasant. He was from Eastern Kentucky and his speech sounded like it. He had a nose that some people normally associate with big drinkers, but George's drinking was pretty moderate at first. He learned his job well and became one of the best operators on our Trick. A Trick was the name used for the teams that worked together. We'd work seven days on the day shift, take four days off, and then four days on the afternoon and evening shift, four days off and then the midnight shift. In our off duty hours we'd attend movies, go down to the club, play ball or anything we could find to do in Korea. George and I got into weight lifting because it was in a recreational building right next to the centralized shower. The recreational equipment wasn't much, but they did have some bar bells and it got to be a contest with us. We built up our lifts pretty good and had out distanced some of the other guys when a true weight lifter showed up one day. He explained what we were doing was risking severe back injuries, so we quit.

I told George all about my family and girl back home and he shared with me. He had gotten married at Christmas time when he went home before shipping out and got daily letters from his wife. One day he told all the guys in the Quonset that he was going to be a papa. For that news we did a little partying. The due date was to be around the first of October, 1956. He was one happy guy and was very faithful with his daily letters home and got pictures of his wife at various stages of her pregnancy. We were all very happy for him and wished that some way he would get to go home, but that wasn't the way the army worked. The baby would most likely be nine months old before George would ever see it.

George had a real German sounding last name. His story was that his ancestors included a Huguenot Soldier that the British brought over to fight the Colonies during the Revolutionary War, but never went back. He stayed, married and raised a family, supposedly in Eastern Kentucky. I thought I could see some of that in his face. He had a rugged face, but one thing George did not lack was intelligence. He liked for people to think he wasn't too smart, but those that fell for that soon found out differently.

One day I came into the Quonset and found George there sitting alone on his footlocker with his head in his hands. Because he had a letter in his hand I immediately thought of bad news from home, maybe to do with the wife and baby. It was about that time. There was no one else in the place when George raised his head and told me the full story. The wife had given birth to twin girls and he had not been notified about it until now, because this letter was from an Attorney saying his wife was divorcing him. The baby girls were black. That one was a hard realization for me to handle. I had seen pictures of his wife, and George was as white as I was almost, so I couldn't fully comprehend what he was saying. George then told me that he had some Negro blood in his past, but he and his family had always passed for white. He attended school with his wife for nearly twelve years and there was never a question, until now. It was not something she wanted to deal with and this attorney was telling how they would proceed.

He did what he could but in Kentucky in 1956 he didn't have much of a chance. The hardship leave under the circumstances was out of the question to the army. George just didn't get much support from anyone. While we still lived together and worked together, he grew angry and started drinking excessively. I know there were times that he went to work half drunk, but he did his job and never got into any trouble for that. He started going down to the local village and spending time down there. The only real trouble he ever got into was when he got drunk and kicked down a wall in one of the houses of ill repute there with his very large boot. I think that cost him some money.

It appears to me now that someone pulled some strings and got this man out of Korea early before he really went off the deep end. I said goodbye to him in the Quonset and wished him well. I never saw George again. When I got back to the states I finished my army career in Virginia. One day we had a G.I. transferred in from a small post in California where I had heard George had ended up. I questioned him as to whether he knew George or not. He shook his head and said George had knifed a guy and was in big trouble when he left.

NOBUKITO, WHERE ARE YOU?

Isn't it strange how some things can stick in your mind that has no relevance to anything? It was in the 5th. Grade that my teacher Mae McClain told us of the Kabuki Plays in Japan. It seems that the actors would dress in strange costumes and do the whole play in an ancient language that no one understood. Why did this come to mind when I arrived in Japan from Korea on a week's R & R (Rest and Recuperation) that I had won as Soldier of the Month in my Battalion?

I checked into the Special Services Hotel for service men in the late afternoon. It seemed like a Palace by comparison to where I had been for the last seven months. It was January 1957 and I had really looked forward to the trip although I knew absolutely no one in Japan and had no agenda. The rooms in the Hotel were three men to a room, so two G.I's were already housed there, but not present, when I arrived. I just sort of hung out in the room until dinner time and went downstairs to see what I could find. I never left the Hotel. I don't know if I found food or not, but there was a bar there.

My drinking experience was very limited. As an athlete I was convinced that one drink would totally destroy me. That and cigarettes, so I stayed away from them all through high school. In basic training I buddied up with a college graduate that was more worldly than I and he introduced me to weakened 3/2 beer they sold on post. It was terrible and easy to resist.

It wasn't until Korea that the old demon got me. The guys I worked with and partied with drank lots of beer. American beer was not their favorite either; they opted for the stronger European beer. I didn't like it very much but in our off hours a lot of time was spent in the club where that is what was going on. I found out early that I had no capacity beyond three, and after finding that out one time, I drank very little.

I sat down at the Hotel Bar in Japan and I was the only one sitting there. A list of drinks hung right on the wall behind the bar. I didn't recognize any of them. I didn't really want the beer, so I chose the one name I could relate to, the Sledge Hammer. When I asked the bartender what was in it he said a little bit of everything. It seemed he put a large variety in my drink. After drinking that one drink, the next thing I knew was waking up the next morning with two roommates sharing my room.

It turned out that my roommates were in the infantry and stationed up on the Demilitarized Zone at the 38th. Parallel. Just a few hundred yards from the North Koreans. They had been lucky they had gotten to Japan before a Red Alert was issued in Korea. Because of tension in the Middle East at the Suez Canal all R and R's had been canceled for the Infantry. When we compared our conditions in our companies, it was clear that their living was much cruder than ours. They were in a defensive mode. Ours was wide open with the crudest part being the 10 hole John in the middle of the compound. That was a shock for the city boys but didn't bother some of the country boys. Theirs had bunkers everywhere. We didn't have to have much armament, because in case of invasion we would be taken out and secured before the women and children. At least that was what we were always told because of our Top Secret Clearances and work. That's funny because the only secret I ever knew was about one of my buddies, but that's another story.

This happened to be their last day in japan and they asked me if I wanted to hang out with them. Two things stand out. We went to this huge theatre showing an American movie. There weren't a lot of people there during the day, but enough Japanese to make me nervous when the battles on the South Sea Islands began. I wonder who ordered that movie? The Americans still won. For the evening they had chosen a fancy night club on the second story down town. I always thought it strange to be upstairs. After we were seated in pretty fancy surroundings, I notice a lot of brass (officers) with women, both American and Asian, in the audience. The floor show began and it wasn't long before I realized that I was seeing my very first strip show. I was embarrassed as I'd peer out the corner of my eye to see how the ladies were reacting. Seemed okay to them, so I took it all in. I guess you could call it my indoctrination for my 20th. Birthday.

The next day I was on my own but the Special Service Club at the Hotel lined me up with a tour of Tokyo. Sitting alone on the bus I was enjoying the guides monologue when a young Japanese man asked if he could sit down beside me and I said sure. Seems he was a friend of the guide and he sometimes would go along on the tours to try to have conversations with Americans. He was a University student and wanted some practical use and help with the English Language. I was happy that he had chosen me. After a couple hour tour he asked if I'd like to meet the next day and see the sights with him. I jumped at the chance. He asked if I had any preference and I went to the depth of my knowledge of Japanese culture and asked if there was a Kabuki Play going on. He said he'd check it out. I have a feeling he had never had that request before.

The next day we started our tour at the Imperial Palace where pictures were taken of him and me. We didn't get to see the Emperor or get inside the walls. Our next stop was a big Museum where I saw the bones of my first dinosaur. I don't know where they found him. We had lunch at a Japanese Restaurant well off the tourist track and I experienced Sukiyaki for the very first time. I fell in love then and there and have never found Sukiyaki that good in the states in sixty years. After that we headed to downtown Tokyo to Ginza Square, a huge market where I bought my girlfriend a Camera. It was then he surprised me by taking me to a small theatre where a Kabuki play was showing. I sat through that play, watching all those painted faces in strange but colorful array, and the language didn't make any difference because I had not gotten by Sayonara in the Japanese language anyway. When I left the theatre my only silent reaction probably was, 'well Mrs. McClain would have been proud of me'.

Out in one street I notice a huge stack of barrels. I was examining them pretty closely and didn't notice the confusion going on behind me. It wasn't until Nobukito came and led me away did I realize that those were barrels of Saki, the Japanese wine, and that I was in the middle of a movie set where a Japanese movie company was filming. So, if you ever see that Movie, look for me. Most likely I made the cutting room floor. I don't know if those barrels were full or not.

That evening we visited a little café and student hangout near his campus and drank soda and enjoyed watching the young students interact. Same as Americans I guess. I couldn't understand them. It had been a long and enjoyable day for me and I think it was the next day that we took the fastest train ride I have ever experienced. The states did not have their type of train at that time and we went from Tokyo to Yokahama in nothing flat to see the Big Budda. The rest of the week wasn't nearly as rememberable. I think Nobukito had to go back to school and I was on my own again. Through the years I've often thought about my private guide who was anxious to learn English. He was doing a good job learning English I thought, and he may have given me a few Japanese words that I no longer have. Through the years I've studied Japanese names showing up in American newspapers and wondered where are you now Nobukito Sato?

TWO WEEKS IN JULY

Operation Chromite, not exactly a household name, was important in winning the Korean War. 75,000 troops on 261 Naval Vessels did an end around attack at Inchon, Korea, cutting off the supplies of the North Koreans who had pushed the South Koreans to the end of the peninsula that is Korea. The date, September 15, 1950.

July 15, 1957. Troops were billeted at Inchon awaiting transportation back to the states. On the eve before they were to board ships they were told they would be unable to take anything that didn't fit into their army issue duffelbag. It seems that the Inchon Harbor does not allow for the landing of troop ships. Smaller landing craft have to transport the soldiers to the bigger ships in the sea and boarding is done by climbing up a cargo net on the side of the ship. It would just be a reversal of what those 75,000 troops did in 1950. There were no piers, or boarding planks, they had to fight from the water onto the beach heads, just like Normandy.

The night before the boarding in 1957 saw several bonfires as things had to be discarded, such as letters from family and sweethearts. That is where I burned 15 months of letters from the girl that I was expecting to see in two weeks. They were right, climbing that cargo net after sitting behind a desk for nearly two years was tough enough. That was one big tall ship with nearly 2000 troops on it when it was full.

The first leg of the trip from Korea was to Japan where more troops were loaded. That leg of the trip went pretty smoothly. There was a scare that the Asiatic Flu was going around and it caught up with us just after leaving Japan. Many of the troops caught it, including me, but if your temperature did not reach 101, you were expected to do the duties assigned you on ship board. Thank goodness I was a guard and didn't get stuck with K.P. duty. My job was standing on the rear of the ship and giving the signal if anyone fell overboard on the midnight shift. About the third night out the assignment changed. One of the soldiers died from the flu and it was my job to guard the body on the bottom deck of the ship. This certainly did not make for an ideal cruise. Thank goodness there were not more.

On the 27th. of July we landed in Seattle, Washington and thank God we could walk off the ship onto a pier. We had to change our clothing for uniforms that were worn state-side as they were different than the issue for Korea. As soon as we had that job done we were free to go home, and I caught the first plane that I could to the Midway Airport in Chicago where my Dad met me. Nothing ever looked any better than the Illinois country side as we traveled the 150 miles to Paris, Illinois. Dad even let me drive his 1957 Oldsmobile but cautioned me that a state speed limit had been passed since I left. Not having the chance to drive any vehicle for almost two years, I was thrilled.

After some rest and finding some civilian clothes to wear, I called my girl. No answer. I failed several times that day to make contact but I kept trying. I had notified her by mail when I expected to get home but maybe she hadn't gotten my letter. When I had about given up I tried one more time and she answered. Seems she had been on vacation in Wisconsin with her family and they cut it short to bring her home. Looking through the glass panes of her front door, I can still see her dancing down the hall to greet me. All the months melted away. Life had changed for the better.

It was the next day that I came to take her to church. I was greeted at the front door by family and told that she wasn't ready yet. I opted to go get some gas in the car and then come back. As I headed back to the car I saw a strange object on the house directly across from her home. When something traumatic happens, the mind gives a surreal message and you don't believe what you are seeing. As I walked toward the triangular T.V. tower running upside the house, it finally dawned on me that I was looking at a little old lady hanging by the neck. About that time a man came out of the next house having seen the same thing and told me to call the police and he would get something to cover her up with. I rushed back to my girl's house and was greeted by her mother and told her of the emergency. Her family all tried to rush to the front of the house but she shushed them to the rear and made the call for me. I went back to help drape a sheet over a tiny little lady who had somehow managed to climb two foot off the ground on the antenna, and hanged herself.

I was twenty years six months old just getting back into the real civilization. It was the strangest two weeks of my life. I went to church that Sunday. I needed it.

PEACE

It was September 2004 when my wife fell and broke her hip out on the street by our apartment. She had been out riding her bicycle and had stopped to talk when she slipped on some loose gravel and went down. She had to have her hip pinned and spent several days in the local hospital. One night after visiting her I was leaving to come home, and when I got to the car I had to lean on it and hold on. Things seemed fuzzy and all seemed darker than usual. This incident scared me into making an appointment with my doctor who referred me to a Cardiologist. He scheduled me for some tests the first week of October. The doctor inserted liquid into my arteries so that he could take pictures showing the flow through my system and heart. Afterwards, I remained in my gown in a bed until the results were in with my wife by my side. When the doctor came in he had a fairly positive attitude. His report was that there seemed to be some blockage but that possibly they could be treated without surgery. He also said that he had asked the heart surgeon to take a look and see if he confirmed his findings.

We waited for another hour or so until heart surgeon showed up with the Cardiologist again. His conclusion was much different. He said the blockages were where the artery made a turn into the heart and that a stint was not going to work in that location. I had two partial blockages and a total blockage in a major vein. Unlike the Cardiologist, this doctor had no bedside manner nor did he pull any punches. He told me right up front that I was a bad risk because of my size, but in his opinion it should be done. My options basically boiled down to medication or surgery. I didn't take long to decide and my wife supported my decision to go ahead with it. The surgery was schedule for October 14, 2004.

In the few days before my surgery I did the usual things of assuring my family and seeing that everything was in order. I can remember that I was at peace. I have been a believer all my life and in the previous thirty years I had grown closer to God and was happy with where my children and wife were also. There were no sleepless nights or anxiety at any time. The Lord had given me peace in my soul, and I was ready if it was my time.

I arrived early on the 14th. at the hospital in the neighboring city for prep work. Somewhere during the prep I was given medication which must have been something to further calm me, whether I needed it or not. My preacher was there to spend time with me and to be with my family, but it wasn't until I was rolling down the hall on my way to surgery that my daughter showed up. She's the one that brought the only tears to my eyes, but they were happy tears at seeing her. They were still rolling down my cheeks when I went into the elevator at about 7:30 a.m. knowing that my family would be well looked after. A brother and his wife had come down from up north to be with them also.

The first thing I remember afterwards was someone trying to put my CPAP on over the oxygen hose that was already in my nose and I was fighting it. I had been on the CPAP for sleeping purposes for ten years and the doctors thought that I should stay on my machine while I was in the hospital. Unfortunately, no one bothered to tell the nurses or the technicians or whoever they were, that it was oxygen or CPAP, not both. The next thing I remembered was visitors in the recovery room at about 6:30 p.m. I was not lucid, but did acknowledge their presence. The next thing was being awakened early the following morning in the recovery room and having to get up and walk. I thought they were crazy, but I did it. Later that day I was taken to a small two person hospital room.

My wife and daughter were both in wheel chairs and there just wasn't room enough where they put me. At this point my wife's sister took over and went to management. She herself worked in a large hospital and knew how to get things done. I ended up in a large single room where I was to remain for the next five days, and where I got excellent care. They actually kept me for two days extra because I had a partial lung collapse and needed treatment. I had a triple heart by-pass surgery and extensive exploration because my dad had died of a heart attack after having a severe back pain. The replacement veins for the by-pass were taken from my left leg above and below the knee.

I returned home on the seventh day although they wanted me to go to rehab in my local hospital. They were not too happy with me when I told them I had a wife recovering from a broken hip and I needed to be at home with her. I would get all the necessary equipment that I needed to rehab there in addition to the home services provided.

About three weeks later I did start with a ten week rehab program at the local hospital as an outpatient. The wife and I both recovered from our surgeries and that special peace has never left me. Through difficult times and good times, my soul is at peace. Each day I awake with a grateful heart, mended by human hands by the grace of God.

TAKE IT, IT'S FREE

The phone rang and my brother was on the line. He asked me if I wanted to go to Vegas with him, free of charge. He had won a trip for two and his friend and future wife did not want to go, so he called me. I wasn't overly busy, so after talking it over with my wife I accepted his generous offer. I had never been to Las Vegas and the bright lights and casino's beckoned me. I was almost sixty years old and had not done anything adventuresome in years.

We were to catch the plane in St. Louis. I lived further south so I picked up my brother early on a Monday morning and drove on in to the Airport where we found a spot in the parking lot and made the gate in time to board our plane. It was an older propeller driven plane that some group in Vegas either owned or leased to bring in their customers. It was crowded and it was noisy. I don't know if all of them had won a free trip to or not, but it was rather uncomfortable for a guy my size, but it wasn't a long plane ride and it was free.

When we walked into the terminal in Vegas the first things we saw were slot machines. They were there for the traveler's convenience if they wanted to pass the time until the hotel buses got around to picking them up. Where I came from you could be arrested for having just one of these machines, and there were dozens just sitting there inviting you to try your luck. I don't recall whether we actually had time for that, but we were soon in our Hotel. Just off the lobby was a vision I had only seen in the movies. Scores and scores of shapes colors and devises very friendly to the eye. We checked in to our free room which was very clean and nice, and developed our strategy for our free trip.

My brother had been to Vegas before and knew how things were. I was a green horn that knew how to play the slots, but had very little knowledge how to do anything else. This was our first day, so rather that venture out to any of the many neighboring hotels, we decided to get our feet wet at our hotel, have a free dinner, and then spend the first evening in. The free food was delicious and unending. After dinner we started out elbow to elbow, but brother decided he wanted to try some of the tables back toward the back, and basically we saw each other the next morning when we woke up. I had determined in my mind that should I lose, it would be limited to the amount of money I had brought with me.

The next day we did the sightseeing in Vegas. We were in and out of several Hotels and Clubs and went down to the Las Vegas strip where all of older original Casinos were. We kept moving doing a little gambling here and there until we ended up at one of the larger Hotels that had poker games going down front and my brother got interested. I was interested but knew I had no business in a poker game in Vegas. I had very little experience and wasn't too sure what the winners where. I knew a Royal Flush was the best, but then what was second best? I watched for a while and the traveled on by myself. We saw each other the following morning.

Included in our free package were two shows. We weren't overwhelmed with what was going in Vegas that week, but ended up seeing a comedian who was fairly well known having been on Carson and other shows. His name was Anderson and he was funny. He even talked to me when I had a coughing spell. I think he offered me some of whatever he was drinking. That might not have been too safe. The other show turned out to be a big production of skates on ice by a big named producer, Frank Lloyd Webber. It was a terrific show but my brother got sick and we had to leave early. On one of the days we took a tourist trip to the Hoover Dam. That turned out to be a lot of walking and step climbing for the out of shape, but was a phenomenal thing to behold with the huge turbines below the dam. How man ever built that structure, I'll never know. That trip was not free.

My brother and I never discussed how we were doing at the tables. I was spending most of my time on the slots with some black jack thrown in. I watched some of the crap tables and roulette tables but could never get up the nerve to try either as it appeared you had to have a system, and I had none. Things just moved too fast for me. Anyway, by the end of my second day I couldn't help but note that most of my money was about gone. Two days of just watching others or staying my room didn't appeal to me, so I took a stab at it and low and behold the Hotel bankers took a check from me. I now had a new supply of cash.

Now I was intent on getting my cash back. I'd play smarter now that I had some experience and get my losses back and then some. One night I was so intent on doing just that and when I looked at my watch it was six a.m. My brother was asleep when I got to the room, and gone when I awoke. This was our last full day in Vegas and I was determined that my luck was going to change. So cashing another check I set out to conquer Vegas once again. I had not been out of the hotel for two days, but they had everything I needed right there.

The next morning we left Vegas but I was still pulling the arm of the bandits almost until the time I walked out the door. Everything was still lit up and the Casino's wide open, so I guessed they had not gone bankrupt. The brother and I didn't discuss how we had made out, but things were pretty quiet on our flight back to Illinois. I for one was really tired from loss of sleep, and maybe he was too. Our free trip was over.

By the time we got our bags and got to the parking lot, it was about ten p.m. Another three hour drive home was ahead for me. I was a little careless when I got into the car in the parking lot and let the door slip and strike the car next to me, just when the owner showed up. I couldn't see any damage in the dark, but he wasn't happy, and he showed that unhappiness by refusing to give our battery a jump when we discovered I had left the lights on. So we spent the next thirty minutes trying to find someone to put cables on our battery and give it a boost to start our engine. It turned out that this was not the first time this ever happened and the Airport did have the service available.

After dropping my brother off at his home, I drove the last sixty miles to my home and was very grateful for two things. First, I was grateful that I got home safe and sound, and secondly I was grateful that my wife never asked me how much I made or lost in Vegas. So if you think I'm going to tell now, you're crazy. I could speculate on my brother's luck also, but I won't. What happens in Vegas, stays in Vegas. I will admit that the trip wasn't free for me.

A TRIP TO NORFOLK

Ever been to Virginia? Parts of it are very beautiful, or at least they were in 1958. That is where the Army sent me to finish my military obligation the last nine months of my enlistment. It was a sharp contrast to my previous fifteen months in Korea. The barracks looked like modern college dormitories and the post like a campus, complete with a nine hole golf course, tennis courts, ball diamonds and gymnasiums and other facilities for hobbies and other sports. The Army part of that post, which incidentally was called Vint Hill Farms because it had been a dairy complete with pastures, was composed of less than two hundred military personnel.

We did the same kind of work there that we had done in Korea, secured by twelve foot fences with barbed wire around our work building. On the way to our unit there was another building also surrounded by barbed wire that only civilians entered into. That was the home of the National Security Agency Headquarters before they got much too big and moved in closer to D.C. There was on post housing for the married and officers, and a small P.X. Life was pretty cozy and easy.

One weekend I decided to visit a friend from high school days who was in the Navy at Norfolk Naval Yards. I had stood up for him to be married the year before and he and his wife had a tiny apartment off base. The biggest event was that we went to see the movie, "The Body Snatchers" which I still see pop up now and again still today. I had a round trip bus ticket and started back to post Sunday evening. It was over 150 miles but I had plenty of time. The bus wasn't too full and somehow I got in a conversation and found that this particular bus was headed to Washington D.C. I questioned the driver and told him I had bought a ticket to Warrenton, Virginia. He said this bus went to Warrenton after it went to D.C., about 75 miles out of the way and into the city. I didn't want to risk another close call for revile as I had done at one other post, so in talking with the driver he suggested that I get off at a highway that would take me to Warrenton more directly. By this time it was about ten in the evening.

It turned out to be a highway, but not a very busy highway. The few cars going my way weren't interested in a young man, and especially since I was not wearing my uniform. I walked a lot and may have caught one ride that helped, but I found myself in Warrenton, Virginia at four a.m. in a diner. I was still twelve miles from my post with only two hour to go. Three rather boisterous guys at one table were just finishing their breakfast and headed out the door when I asked them where they were headed. They said they worked construction in D.C. and were headed there this Monday morning. I told them my dilemma and they told me to hop in. They were going my way. It was a big car, maybe even a sporty Cadillac. They left that parking lot in a hurry with me in the back seat and I heard one guy tell the other to see what she'd do. When the count went over 100 I quit listening. Just held my breath. It wasn't long until they stopped and said here is where you wanted out. Somehow I got my legs to hold me up and started the walk back toward the post. I still had four miles along a beautiful tree lined two lane highway. Other than a gap in the trees where in the daylight you could see wheat fields, this was the scenery. I was plodding along when I was picked up by a soldier who lived off post and was making his way to work. I ended up with time to get a quick shower and shave before breakfast and another days work. I hope no secrets slipped by me that day.

That was about the time that the Sputnik was launched by the Russians and we would trace its signal around the world. Our equipment could pick up that needle in the haystack, if it moved. I looked it up recently. Vint Hill Farms Army Post is no more. They must have discovered it looked more like a country club and converted it for the higher ups. If they had promised me duty there for 20 years I might have re-enlisted. That is if Marilyn would have let me. By then she was calling the shots.

NOTHING TO BE PROUD OF

I was still just eighteen and a long way from home, but things happen. It was a Wednesday before Thanksgiving 1955 when I learned that some guys in my company were headed back to Illinois for the holiday by automobile. It was well over the limits on our pass, but if they were going, for a little gas money I could too. It was a bit of a risk to travel those highways through that terrain from Massachusetts in late November, and it was a thousand miles, but boys would be boys. We took off on Wednesday after schooling and by the time it was dark on Thursday we were in Illinois.

Why did I, not a usual risk taker, take this one? Well first, I wanted to see my Dad and several siblings that were still in the area. But whose kidding who, I went home to see Marilyn, the girl I had gone steady with for a year in high school and whom I'd broken up with before I graduated. The last time I had been home in August I date three different girls and had been writing two regularly from Massachusetts, Marilyn and Carolyn. Only after I found out that they sat next to each other in Speech class did I change that. I decided I'd rather concentrate on Marilyn. We had made no commitments, but I wanted to see her very much. I don't remember making contact with her that evening, but I did on Friday and spent considerable time with her before starting back to the post of Saturday. She would soon be off to college and I would be away for months, but we felt pretty strong connections but knew we had to go our separate ways and date others. I went back to the Army feeling very good about our relationship, but was carrying one guilt that I still have not forgotten.

When I had gotten to Fort Devens at Ayer, Massachusetts in late August 1955, I was fancy free. I had enjoyed my fifteen day leave at home for the most part, but now faced a much different life. We had the post theatre, the U.S.O. just outside of the post in Ayer, and of course the heavily populated communities of Mass. On a private's salary, you were limited. Movies cost a quarter and the U.S.O. cost nothing. You even got free refreshments and entertainment at times. One night a week there would be dancing and the local girls came in and mixed with the guys. Not a bad set up. They knew we had little money and they were just there to have some fun themselves.

After several weeks of going into town, I decided to try the dance with some of the buddies and got up enough nerve to ask a girl to dance. From that experience I was taught how to Polka and I found that dancing was lots of fun. Some high school girls had taught me to Jitterbug my senior year, so I was better off than some of my buddies. Dancing is how I met Angie Campanello. She was short, a little stout, and a couple of years older than I. She looked Italian. As dances would come around, I found myself paired with her more and more often. She was a little quiet but nice. I never saw her outside of the U.S.O. but got to know some of her girlfriends too and I had fun going to the weekly dance.

That was the status the week before Thanksgiving. Angie asked me what I was doing for the holiday and I had no plans. She asked if I'd like to come to her family's home in Worcester, Mass. for dinner. I thanked her very much and said I would. She went to great lengths to draw me a map on how to get to Worcester and how to find her home. I felt good that I was not just going to be confined to the post eating Army turkey that day. But, that was before I heard of a ride to Illinois.

When I had definite plans to come to Illinois, to my credit I tried to call her. I didn't know her parents name and Worcester was probably one of the bigger cities in Massachusetts, so you know how many Campanello's lived there? I ended up not making any contact with anyone and the chair set for me at the table was probably not filled. Afterwards, when the next dance night at the U.S.O. came around I stayed in the barracks. No guts. It was a few weeks before I ventured to dance night again, but I stayed in the shadows. I saw Angie at a distance a time or two, but we never spoke. Dances became less fun and I started concentrating on the little girl I left behind. I would never want to feel guilty about standing her up.

TEACHERS, I HAD A FEW MORE

After the elementary years where you were basically exposed to one teacher for the entire day and school year, high school was a major change. This was where you sat in a teacher's classroom for about fifty minutes then moved on six or seven times a day. You had multiple teachers and they in return had about 200 different students per day instead of 25. It was quite an adjustment. Teachers, I had all kinds. Some of them kind and some of them not so kind. Some of them in the business out of love. Some to make a living. Some were very sharp and some of questionable intellect.

I guess my biggest exposure was to the gym class teachers who were also coaches. I got to know them best, although all my coaches did not have gym classes. Mr. Stevens taught math and Mr. Stabler and Mr. Heron taught history. I didn't have either of them for history. I got unlucky and got the golf coach Mr. Johnson. I didn't play golf and I didn't wear tailored shirts and sharp shoes and socks. They were important to Mr. Johnson. My grades showed that.

One of my teachers was Mr. Eveland and he had the biggest impact on my life of all of my teachers. He taught gym and driver's education. He coached cross country, basketball, and track. I think he could have taught other things too as I never doubted his basic intelligence, but it just so happened he did what he did best, coached. He was there day one of my high school years and every day for all four years. He had assistants coaching the freshman and sophomore squads, but he still had hands on interest and you knew he was watching to see that the job was being done right. He was well respected by everyone. Well most everyone.

My brother Aaron and Coach Eveland were not on the proper wave length from the very start. Aaron transferred in as a six foot two junior ball player with high expectations. Let's just say that both parties were a little hard headed and couldn't always agree. This got worse until they had a real altercation and brother Aaron was through playing ball for Mr. Eveland. He won his varsity letter but knew he'd not be welcome back his senior year. While this was going on, I was being treated just fine and got considerable encouragement. Even after I missed my sophomore year playing ball because of the death of my mother, Coach Eveland welcomed me back as a junior and gave me every opportunity, but the year off didn't help me. I basically got an unearned varsity letter, but the main thing I got was a caring coach there to guide me. He knew I had lost my mother and was living in difficult circumstances so he'd personally instructed me for my health and other hygiene questions which were helpful.

Then there was Miss Addie Hochstrasser, an elderly English teacher who only had time for the sharply dressed students who were the white color citizenry sons or daughters, and in some cases the daughters of a school board members or local doctors. She normally just taught Senior English for college prep students, but my junior year they scheduled her to teach junior literature also. I can truthfully say that I did not earn one smile from that lady all year. It wasn't a very pretty smile, but at least it would have shown some friendliness.

Things got worse when basketball season began and carried through track season that year. When there would be an out of town game, quite often we would have to leave our classes a little early to make the trip. It just so happened that Miss Hochstrasser's class was the last one of the day, and I was the only basketball and track player in the room. We'd be advised to tell our teacher when we had to leave early, and usually they'd excuse us at the proper time. Not Miss Hochstrasser. When I'd try to draw her attention to the time, she would ignore me. Not until Mr. Eveland would show up at the door would she excuse me, normally with the remark that I had not told her. That wasn't true and fortunately the Coach had been around long enough to know it. Even when she would excuse me on time, it was with the ugliest scowl.

Let's just say, if I had had to take Miss Hochstrasser's college prep English my senior year, or if I had had two or three Miss Hochstrasser's in my high school, I would have been a drop out. I'll never forget when the word of Miss Hochstrasser's death was announced at about our 25th. Class Reunion. I was surprised at the glowing tributes from our class president, and the doctor's daughter, and the straight A students. Many of us just remained silent. I will say that my wife doesn't necessarily agree with my view. She was a class behind me and never expressed any feelings for Miss Hochstrasser, positive or negative, but of course she had known Marilyn's parents ever since she came to town in the thirties. Could have had some bearing.

That is pretty sad when you write about the teachers you've had and you end up on a note like that. I didn't even mention the wonderful Principal that I had, Mr. Jenkins. He took me under his wing and helped me make it through those last two and a half years as did Mr. Eggleston, Mr. Gibson, Mrs.

Kendrick, and the other coaches. And then of course there were a few more.

SUPPORTING P.B.S.

Since the day when my three children sat quietly in front of the T.V. watching Ernie and Big Bird and then Mr. Roberts and several others, I've been beholden to the Public Broadcasting System. It gave us wholesome programming and relatively peace and quiet around the house. In my coming and going I saw very little of what was going on, but it served an important purpose for my wife also. She had time to fix the meals. For this a modest donation seemed fair.

As the years passed and the quiet time was no longer needed around the house, P.B.S. got less attention with only an occasional view. Sometimes an independent news cast was nice, but that seemed to erode a bit, but also they brought on more and more sports telecast of the S.I.U. sports, and the donations continued. Not a lot, but I did my part for keeping the programming on the air.

Then one day in about 1990 I was hard up for entertainment and was flipping around the channels and landed on P.B.S. It was showing a gentlemen painting landscapes. I watched with interest as he explained every stroke in a quiet voice with a lilt, very pleasant. In thirty minutes time he created a masterpiece. It looked so easy and the scenes he painted from photos were my kind of pictures. They were country landscapes and old barns and buildings. They did not have people, animals, or equipment. I was amazed at his talent, because since my youngest years I had not been able to create any drawing that anyone would recognize. My art talents did not exist, but he sold the idea that even I should try anyway.

So the following week I sat posed in front of the T.V. I started small with a couple of cheap brushes and three or four small tubes of paint, and butcher paper. I didn't have much luck but was learning his method of mixing and overlaying in a way that was beautiful. Each week I would add to my collection with a pallet board and I think my wife bought me my first easel. I was ready for the big time. I started taking pictures of things around our two acre farm and over the fence. I scoured magazines for outstanding landscapes that I wanted to duplicate. Each week I got more and more addicted. I even signed up with a lady from my church that gave classes in her basement once a week. I sat there for 8 or 10 weeks with the other ladies taking it all in. At first I was a little taken back that I was the only male, but Opal my teacher encouraged me and kept me going.

After several weeks, painting on a Masonite board, I finally created my first master piece that hangs on my wall to this day with my initials in the bottom corner. To me, that river through the valley with the mountains in the background should be in an Art Institute somewhere. I wouldn't tell them that it was a 75% Opal creation as she stood over my shoulder showing me how to get the job done and often using my brush to illustrate the right way. After that I couldn't stop painting.

The expenses increased as I graduated to canvas and frames and many hues of color. The first canvases had many do overs until I eventually got keepers. After I filled up my own home to the extent the wife would allow, I started favoring the siblings. I only had seven of them but they were all blessed with an original landscape painting by their artist brother. I would paint a picture for anyone and frame it, and this went on for four years until we moved back to town and I no longer had the country landscape to inspire me. My addiction wore off and I stopped. I got into helping my daughter write her biography and painting was forgotten. Ten years later when I tried to revive my artistic ability, it had all been forgotten.

With that gone, I was back to P.B.S. I officially retired at sixty-five from my business. By then I had the golf addiction, but you couldn't do that all the time, especially in the winter. One day I was watching P.B.S. and there was a guy demonstrating how to learn to cord on the piano. I've always loved music and have a pretty good ear for it. My mother tried to interest me in the piano when I was twelve, but it couldn't compete with the outside and the ball playing. This guy caught my attention so I sat down to watch.

At age seventy I invested in a fifteen dollar compact disc that had all the information that I would need to learn to play the piano in ten days. Seemed fair to me. For this I would still keep my donations to Public Broadcasting going. In less than ten days, on a ninety dollars electric keyboard, I was yelling at my wife, 'dear come hear this'. She got tired of my calling but did agree that a used piano may be something we could buy. I wore that piano out and we invested in a beautiful new piano. It wasn't just me, the wife could play some when I was sleeping or playing golf.

I finally went public with a little playing for a small church group, and then I started playing weekly for the local Nursing Home. I'd arrive at four p.m. and play while they entered the dining room for dinner. I had put together over 400 hymns, pop music, and holiday music that I could play by ear, but some of the people asked to hear the same ones week after week which was okay. Some of the audience slept, some talked, and some listened, but I got enough encouragement to continue on for almost four years until my arthritis and inability to sit on a piano bench for an extended period of time got to me. I didn't want to quit, but I had to. I'm told I was missed and I missed them. I had grown accustomed to many of their faces.

One of my talents left me and another has waned because I can't play as much as I used to. But I still love it. Both gave me enjoyment literally for years. Look around when you're out. You may be seeing a D.R.S. masterpiece. I don't know where my entire painting creations are now as five of my siblings have died, but I know two have burned. The others were probably fought over in estate battles.

Anyway, the seed to give both a try started with the local P.B.S. T.V. station that played a big part in my finding a talent. For that, I will always be grateful and my support for the Public Broadcasting System will continue.

ONE SPUDNUT PLEASE

You can say all you want about some of the delicious donuts on the market today, but if you never had a spudnut, you haven't lived. They used to be on major college campuses but have disappeared now. I know it wasn't because they weren't the best; the cost must have entered into the equation. My last memory of one was on the Southern Illinois Campus in about 1985.

What was a spudnut? It looked like a donut but was made with potato flour. I believe the manufacturing facility was in Utah and the product was shipped nationwide in fifty pound bags. You just measured the flour, added the right amount of water and yeast and stirred in a large pot for a fixed period of time. It was then allowed to rise, punched down two times, and then taken out and cut into loaves and kept warm until it was needed. It would then be rolled out with a large roller and then cut with a donut cutter by hand. It was then put back in the oven for it to rise again before putting them in boiling oil. After that they were either glazed over or dipped into any one of the many icings available. If you were really lucky, you might hit the timing just right and get a warm one to go with your coffee, milk, or juice. It was unbeatable.

There was a cake donut too called a spuddie. This was a moist flour concoction that was put into a dispensing device that dropped a perfectly formed cake donut in the deep fryer. Again, this was dipped in any choice of icing known to man. It wasn't my favorite, but for those who liked the cake variety, it was great.

The operations did not stop there. When round donuts were cut from the spudnut flour, there were always edges that did not get used. Enough of these saved could be made into twists or persians. Sometimes extra dough had to be run just for this product as they became more popular. We all know what a twist is, but a persian was the name given to the cinnamon roll. Depending on the cutter, this could be the size of nicely cut big cookie, or about the size of the average dinner plate. The boss would not be too happy at the latter. They did have their benefits though. In a twenty four hour operation, knowing that hot persians might be available the size of a hub cap in the middle of the night kept both the city and campus police coming by, thereby securing the premises.

On the campus at the University of Illinois there were two such shops making and selling spudnuts. Both were owned by Herman Trapp who was an old ex semi-pro football player who played for George Halas of Chicago Bear fame when he had the Decatur Staleys. Mr. Trapp was rough but fair. He was semi-retired with his son-in-law running the business, but Fred needed help from him often. The shop on the Champaign side of campus was open about fourteen hours a day to serve the students. My wife waited counter and did dishes there for a while.

The shop on the Urbana side of campus was open 24 hours a day, seven days a week. It served both the students but also the Greek Houses, dorms and the Chanute Air Force Base in Rantoul up the road. This meant a major production every night that involved about five guys working just as fast as they could making and boxing product. For two years I was one of those guys working from eleven to seven, working the counter, making the product, and getting the delivery men on their way. For this, most of the time I made $1.00 per hour and got all I could eat.

The shops are no longer there. I don't know when they left. I just know that somehow that product should be available to us today. It's very healthy. I ate it for dinner every night and breakfast every morning, six day a week, and look at me. There are very few of you out there that don't like potatoes in one form or another. Well I'm telling you that this was one great form.

My spudnut story does not have a happy ending. After about a year I graduated to cutter on the Saturday night shift. This meant that I was the boss of that shift so the night manager could have a night off. For one night I was responsible for everything and got paid $1.50 per hour. During finals week at the end of my second year, on a Sunday morning I got off work and went home and sacked out. About three hours later Mr. Trapp called and said I'd forgotten to drain the fryer and clean it. The truth was, I had run out of time. He instructed me to get right back in there and do it. I told him I needed my sleep so I could study for finals for the next day before I had to report in for work that night. He said that I could either get in there or pick up my last check. He was right, the cleaning the fryer was my responsibility, but after two years I think my time had come to an end and I told him I'd be in on Monday to get my check. I did get a full nights rest that night before starting my finals, but I don't know if it helped any or not. I just know that was the only time I was ever fired from a job, except when I was six and fudged a little picking tomatoes.

CAN YOU FIND A DIME?

What would you do for a dime? Better yet, what would you do for fifty cents? I saw that demonstrated best in 1970.

In April 1968 I was hired by Borg Warner to be the Controller of the Washer Plant of the Norge Company in Herrin, Illinois. It was a big manufacturing operation and my responsibility was a department of two dozen personnel involved in general accounting, cost accounting, payroll, data processing, data collection, and cost estimating. Since I had passed my C.P.A. test in 1966, my resume got more attention and I had progressed well. I wasn't quite sure of my future when Borg Warner sold the Norge Division to an entity I had never heard of less than three months later. Let's just say that Fedders Corporation was no Borg Warner. The plant employed from 1300 to 1800 employees the years I was there, and we faced many different challenges.

One of the men under me, the cost estimator, had a very important job. When product development would come up with a new idea, especially one involved in a possible cost savings, his job was to run the figures and make the comparisons. He would work with design, engineering, and whomever he needed to in the process. Cost savings was a very big deal in the appliance business because the competition was so tough. Over half of the Norge production was the Signature Brand for Montgomery Ward, and if Wards could get it cheaper elsewhere, the Norge operation would be in serious trouble.

I didn't normally get involved in the day to day estimating, but when my man needed support or back up, it was my job to chime in. One such project was a proposed savings on the corner posts in the shipping carton. Product Development had come up with a new design that my man had put a cost saving of fifty cents per carton. For a product that cost just over a hundred dollars to build in 1970, that was considered to be substantial. The problem is that the Engineers would not allow it. That is what got the management team involved. The existing posts were designed to have a substantial safety zone when the product would be stacked in warehouses. It appeared to be about twice of what was necessary and the Vice President of Engineering was adamant about it remaining right there. Once I had verified the accuracy of my cost estimator's work, I stood firm on what the saving would be. The proposed post still had a substantial safety margin and the debate went on. The local Vice President of Manufacturing with the support of his home office superior finally made the decision. The new product year would have the re-designed corner post. Our Vice President of Engineering, Carl Knerr, just hung his head. I thought he was going to cry.

The following September the new product was filling up the warehouses waiting for the holiday shipments to begin. The line had worked overtime and a good year was expected. In addition to the Signature Brand and the Norge Brand, there were three or four other lesser known brands also. Production had been about two thousand units per day for four to six months and the fifty cents saving clicked off on each one, until one weekend in September. The units stacked four and five high in the warehouses started toppling over as the corner post gave way to the weight exerted on them. Once they started toppling, no man could stop them and before they finished, thousands of washers had hit the concrete floors.

Each damaged carton had to be opened and diagnosed for damage. All had to be re-cartoned and many had to go through special repair lines set up with special teams of workers. Especially vulnerable was the transmission. I don't think Mr. Knerr, the V.P. of Engineering ever told the other guys, 'I told you so', but he might have asked product development and others if they had fifty cents to lend him.

IT CAN STILL WORK!

I grew up in Paris, Illinois. I lived in the northeast part of town in a nice clean neighborhood. Living in the south end of town was a family that had dirt floors in their home. There were a lot of run down homes in that area. I only knew of this family because there were three boys that I got to know in high school. In the earlier years I only knew one slightly but heard of them through my cousin who also lived in the south end.

The two younger ones had personalities befitting guys who had grown up on hard times and were defensive because they were looked down on by others. They were hard to get to know. The older one had grown through that stage of life and was a very popular with his fellow students and was well known for his participation in sports. The younger two had problems with authority, and the youngest who was my age did not graduate with my class. By our senior year he had become more popular but still had a way to go in getting along with people. I understand that he did get to graduate by taking an extra year of schooling.

I graduated from high school and went on my way to the military and then to college. I didn't know what had happened to the guys and because we were never close, they never crossed my mind. A few years later you can imagine my surprise when I heard that the middle boy, two years my senior, was teaching math at my old high school. Who would have thought that he would have continued on to college and accomplished that feat? Apparently he had more going for him intellectually that I realized. It did make me wonder what had happened to the brother my age.

Another twenty years passed and I was living in Herrin, Illinois in my own business. One of my clients and friend had his own business and one day he happened to mention that his daughter was moving back to Herrin. She was a Social Worker in Special Education in the school system, as was her husband. My friend told me his son in law was from Paris, Illinois. My jaw dropped when I found out his name. It was the same guy who didn't graduate with my class, and seemingly had little chance for a future. He like his brother was a college graduate with an advanced degree. I met him and renewed our acquaintance, but we never really became more than acquaintances. He and I had most of our discussions about our classmates when we'd meet at the golf course which he loved to play, and was very good at.

One day he revealed to me the success that his older brother had in the east. Although he either had or was close to retirement, he had an executive position with a conglomerate owning several successful banks in the Virginia or North Carolina area and was very wealthy. This brought to a closure what I knew of three boys who started out in a shack with dirt floors and no visible opportunity to get ahead in America. I know where I started, but the fact that all three of them would succeed is an amazing story to me. I don't know anything about their parents and whether they witnessed this change for them, but here are three guys who pulled themselves up by the boot straps, and often they barely had wearable shoes. That was in the 1950's in America, and it can still work.

THE UNEXPECTED

Many things arise in one's life that we could call unexpected. This story relates to my life in politics. A period from 1976 to 1984. That is a period in my life that was unexpected even by me earlier in my life. Public office had never crossed my mind until 1976. At that time I became an unexpected candidate for Treasurer of a community, Herrin, Illinois, population 10,000. I lost. That was not unexpected by most people as I had only lived in the community for eight years.

Politics was not on my mind as I was trying to grow my own business and give my young family what they needed for the next four years. I didn't expect it to take so long for my business to make a living for us when I opened the doors the first day of January in 1972, but it had. In 1980 I got the bug to try to unseat the current Mayor who was running for re-election. He was the first Italian American Mayor of a community that had many a second generation families that came over from Italy to work the coal mines of Southern Illinois. In a hard fought election that turned out more voters than had ever cast a vote for the Mayor's job before or since, the unexpected happened. I won by about 50 votes.

I had no agenda but to try and run the cities operation in a businesslike manner. It was a community that had seen a lot of cronyism in the past and under the table dealings. In fact the Mayor for eight years from 1969 to 1977 had just been imprisoned for kickbacks along with two other city officials. The townspeople were ready for a change and unexpectedly elected a newcomer who moved to town in 1968 with his family.

When I took office some unexpected things happened. First, one of the aldermen that ran with me on my ticket started trying to make deals right away and became one of my biggest adversaries right from the start. Surprisingly I had department heads quit because they just assumed that they would be replaced by me automatically. In fact, the only person I planned to replace was a position where I knew the person the best. I liked her but she had trouble getting along with the existing aldermen and they wanted her replaced. She had been a political appointee of my predecessor.

One of my pet projects was getting a movie reopened in the community for the youth. I was having a hard time finding financing from the private sector when I learned of a long standing fund that was controlled by the bank and inactive for several years. I tried to make the case to use some of those funds for the movie unsuccessfully and was rather upset at the town fathers for their lack of support. On the side, one of them came and gave me a check for the project but made his case for why those funds should not be used for a movie project. That was unexpected and I appreciated his taking the time and putting his money where his mouth was. In the end, the project was not successful because of lack of community interest and I had to let it die.

Beside my political life, I was an Elder in my Church. One of my fellow Elders attempted to complicate my efforts to run for public office. That was unexpected. During this period I heard one of the past Elders of my Church trying to justify some horrible things that had happened in my community back in the 1920's. That dumb founded me. Coal miners brought in to work the mines when the local miners went on strike were gathered up and murdered. He tried to show some justification for that. Also unexpected was the strong support and encouragement that I got from the Priest of the local Catholic Church. He was the one who would stop in periodically and give me a boost or write a favorable article supporting me. He was there in the last months of my term when my own father died feeling my grief. As a protestant, this was unexpected.

I resigned before the end of my four years. I didn't expect to do that but I lost heart when a newly elected group of aldermen came in with the idea of just opposing me instead of doing what was right for the community. It was unexpected when the area newspaper wrote an editorial supporting me and saying I was responsible for breaking up the politics as usual in my community. This was the same paper that opposed my election in the first place, but came to support me when I did the unexpected.

HERE HE IS

I have to admit that for as long as I can remember, I always wanted to be center noticed. I think that was brought on by being the youngest and not given much attention. Another way of putting that might be I wanted to be noticed or not overlooked. The fact is, I'd want the attention and then my nerves would take over and I'd be miserable trying to control them. Sometimes I would and sometimes I wouldn't keep my nerves in check.

Because I am no 'cool hand Luke', I've embarrassed myself at different times. Once in a while I got center stage and made out okay. I guess the times that happened about offset the times it didn't happen. The one time that it didn't happen was probably my last major boo boo in my public life.

Following my inclination to be in the spotlight, in 1981 I ran for and was elected mayor of my community of Herrin, Illinois. Basically I was an outsider that pulled an upset over an incumbent lifelong resident. We did not run on the usual party lines although my community was normally in the Democrat column. My inclinations were more to the Republican side but this never came up in the election. I was elected for a four year term and never intended to ever run for re-election because I had my own business and was trying to make a living at the same time.

The saying goes that sometimes in politics you make strange bedfellows. To say that I never compromised my beliefs would not be true. I had definite things I wanted to do, but there were times when I had to give a little to get a little. For the most part I was able to hold out on my principles and do the right thing. It was a part time commitment but I wanted to make my years in office count.

When a neighboring unincorporated community came to see me for some help in my second year, I listened to them. The community known as Number 9 was trying to get a grant from the state for a community building for their citizens. Their story and reasoning seemed legitimate enough to me so I wrote a letter detailing my support for their project. The community of about 250 people was about ninety five percent Afro-American. Their efforts were being opposed by a small village adjoining Number Nine, but at the same time they would not incorporate them as it would upset the balance of power in the village opposing their efforts. This had gone on for years. Through several twist and turns I aided their efforts until the grant was finally awarded them. In fact the governor was coming to town to hand it to them personally.

Governor Jim Thompson was known as a powerful Republican in the State for many years. Being from the Chicago area, he ranked pretty high on the national scene also. When the word came that he'd be coming down, the leaders of Number Nine came to me and said they wanted me to be in attendance and have the honor of introducing the Governor at the special meeting called for that purpose. I didn't hesitate and said yes I gladly would.

The largest building in Number Nine was a church that could probably hold a hundred people, and it was jammed. I got there early and was seated on the raised platform. The Governor was late and I just passed the time of day with the head of their assembly. The Governor finally rushed in with two or three assistants and was seated without any introductions or anything. The head of the Assembly then went to the podium and introduced me, the Mayor of Herrin, Illinois who was instrumental in helping Number Nine in their grant application. By this time my nerves were working and I walked up to the podium, they had no need for a microphone in their small building, and said in a shaky voice, "I'd like to introduce the Governor of the State of Illinois" and sat down. Governor Thompson looked at me a little strange and took over. After he was done he shook the hand of the Assemblies head and left as quickly as he had arrived.

He didn't thank me for the introduction. I expect he was use to more glowing remarks about himself and his position, but I never said I was a politician. In truth, the nerves got to me. Maybe that was part of the reason I resigned as Mayor with a little over a year left to give my business my full attention. If I'm going to embarrass myself, I'd rather not do it so publicly. So far, so good.

HAIL TO THE CHIEF

Two men manned the gatehouse. First they checked to see if I was on the list they had and that I had the proper identification. Then I walked through the machine to sensor if I had any significant metal on me. Only then was I directed which path I was to follow and which door I was to enter. I really just had to follow the stream ahead of me going the same place, the Yellow Room at the White House.

To this day I don't know why my name was on the invitation list to go hear the President speak at the White House. Of the couple of hundred persons attending, I was only one of two Mayors from the State of Illinois. All of the attendees were elected officials at different levels of government. Illinois probably had a total of less than ten. As the room filled up, you could see all of the cameras in the back and some familiar faces that you could see nightly on your television.

It was the summer of 1982 and when the invitation came, the local banks put together a fund so that I wouldn't need to use my own or city funds to make the trip. With a couple of weeks to plan, I asked the more experience members of our community about what exactly I could accomplish on such a trip. They gave me ideas, among them to visit HUD, Housing Urban Development, to see if housing money was available for building more units for the homeless and I made an appointment with our State Senator to try and score some points with him. There were some other ideas that I don't recall, but I had an agenda after the White House.

Of course we all rose and applauded when President Ronald Reagan entered the room waving and smiling. That man really appeared genuine. He spoke to us for about thirty minutes on economic development and other things and it was more or less him trying to rally the troops. I know I was ready. He took plenty of time for questions from the floor but the reporters tried to dominate that period and afterwards he shook many hands, apparently in no hurry. I was raised not to bother people and I couldn't make myself get into that line to shake the man's hand. It was just an intrusion and he did have more important things to do. I did make eye contact with him a couple of times and got a warm smile, but I just wanted to say, let the man go, enough is enough.

I walked out of that place with the highest admiration for that man and I've never lost it. From there I hit the streets to find these large office building housing all of those important departments. I actually got to talk to a couple of people but I suspect they were not too high on the pecking list and nothing ever came of it.

The old but palatial hotel that I was staying in was within eye sight of the White House. I wasn't seeing the front view, but I could see it from my window. I had an early morning appointment to see Senator Paul Simon, but after dinner I had a message in my box that his office had called and regrettably canceled the meeting. Priority items had come up. I had met and talked to Paul a couple of times in Herrin when he would come and visit. I assisted him in getting a place in our City Hall to hold a meeting one time. I liked Paul even though he was a liberal Democrat and I believe he would have met with me had more important things not have come up. So, the next day I caught the plane back home. I had been to the White House. I had seen the President at very close range, and I found we had lots in common. We were both from Illinois. We both had loving mothers and fathers, but the fathers had a tendency to drink a little too much. We both had families and we were both were once actors. I had been in the Junior Class Play of 'State Fair'. How many people can say that along with Hail to the Chief.

THE ROAD TO INDEPENDENCE

In 1940 I was quite young. Perhaps my parents voted in the election that year when Franklin Delano Roosevelt was up for his third term, but I sincerely doubt it. Getting to the polls in town from the country wasn't that easy and if it meant missing a day in the fields, that wouldn't be good. Dad would probably have liked to vote against the man who was in office when the family farm was lost, but I'll never know. For some reason and at some point my Dad became a dye in the wool Republican voting only straight tickets. He told one of his nephews one time that was running for office in another part of the state, that if he ever wanted his vote he'd have to change parties. He never changed that view to the very end.

As for me, I think that in 1944 I may have gone for F.D.R. He was the man that I saw most in the newsreels in the movies and he seemed okay to me. I don't know who his opponent was. In 1948 I was a Truman supporter. This was the man whose train slowed coming through Paris and he waved to me from the Caboose where I was sitting and folding newspapers waiting for him. The Republicans might have persuaded me had they not run a beady eyed New Yorker with a thin mustache. Harry won and I was happy. At the age of eleven I didn't really hear what Dad had to say about it, and my mother could care less about politics.

1952 was a different story though. When fellow warrior Ike ran for president, there was no doubt who I would support. He beat a fellow Republican by the name of Bob Taft in the primary and I'm glad he did. Mr. Taft didn't appear too much different than Mr. Dewey from New York. As far as the Democrats, they said Mr. Stevenson was from Illinois, but I never saw him here. Mr. Barkley from Kentucky seemed like a nice enough grandfather figure, but in the final analysis, Ike was the man.

By the 1956 election I was still an ineligible voter, because of age, sitting in my company compound near Seoul, Korea. Ike was still okay by me but I'll have to admit that the Democratic Ticket with Estes Kefauver running for vice president in his coonskin hat had a certain flair about him. Mr. Stevenson was still from Illinois, but I still had never seen him. To be fair, I had never seen Ike either, but you have to take in account that he was in Europe fighting a war for a long time. Adlai wasn't.

It was sometime between 1956 and 1958 that I began to get correspondence from my fiancée's grandmother. We had met a few times and she was very dear. At the time she was probably about seventy-eight years old and she sent me a book written by John Kennedy. In her letter she mentioned that she thought this man would make an excellent president. I think I knew enough at the time to realize that he was a Democrat, but I had an open mind. Ike couldn't run again and his vice president Nixon was an unknown as far as I could tell. He was from California and I had never seen him.

By the 1960 campaign I was married and on the University Campus in Champaign, Illinois when candidate John Kennedy spoke to the students. Marilyn and I stood about fifty yards away and listened to his well-rehearsed speech. It was good. Marilyn and I were eligible to cast our first vote ever in politics. Grandmother had made her thoughts known and all I knew of my father in law's politics was that you didn't say Republican in his presence. My dad was about as bad and he left no doubt what his son should do. Now you have to understand that I grew up in an Apostolic household where Catholicism was a bad word. In 1960 they still ate fish on Fridays and frequented the clubs closely associated with their Church where forbidden drinks were sold. They may still do that one. In the end result I voted for Nixon and assumed my wife did also as we'd only been married two years. We had seen John in person and still let him down.

1964 was an off year for presidential elections. Can you remember any year when the candidates looked so unpresidental. Johnson versus Goldwater. Johnson gave a speech a year or two earlier at my sister in laws graduation. Even so, I couldn't get past those eyes and the fact that he was from Texas. There are still times when I think that Texas and

Chicago should form their own country and move out. Let's just say that I convinced myself that Barry was the lesser of two evils, but he lost anyway.

The comeback ex V.P. was there in 1968, ready to roll for the Republicans. I had wasted a vote on him once and I still had not seen him in person. His opponent Hubert Humphrey had a happy demeanor and seemed very likeable. We happily voted for him but he lost. We now had a record of 3 presidential votes with no winners, but we were voting for the man, at least in two out of three cases.

I voted for the winner in 1972 who turned out to be a loser, but he didn't have an opponent. Nixon would still have beaten him in a landslide without the cheating that he did. I was happy to see Gerald Ford take over.

By this time my voting pattern had evolved at every level. The presidential votes, except for Humphrey, had been for Republicans because they best represented my views. But I have voted for democrats for state and local offices many times. I've registered as a Democrat and voted in several primaries. I did that so I could vote for Paul Simon in 1988. Unfortunately he didn't make it to the national ticket. I was almost persuaded by my daughter to go for Jimmy Carter in 1980, but at the last minute Ronald Reagan came to Herrin to visit us and I stood less than twenty feet from him. Jimmy didn't show up but my daughter still loved him. A few years later we got off the beaten path to visit his home town in Plains, Georgia.

I didn't take too long on the road to independence. I have always listened to the man first and foremost. Now that there are also women in the race, I find it refreshing to hear honest women expound on their ideas for America. One strong criteria is that they have to be honest and trustworthy. I don't know how many more votes I will have, but if I can show up and vote, it will be as an Independent.

THE PROGRESSIVE PARTY

This political party formed in 1980 in Herrin, Illinois never really got off the ground. Maybe if it had we wouldn't have the mess that we have in Washington today. What this country really needs is a viable third party. Well, it's not my fault, I tried.

Knowing nothing about politics, I formed a party to unseat the incumbent Mayor of the city of Herrin, Illinois. He was a nice enough old guy but with him it was politics as usual. Appoint your friends and sit back and watch. He had defeated another mayor four years earlier who ended up going to the Penitentiary, so Herrin was not known for its above board dealings.

It was customary to put together a slate that would run together. My slate only consisted of three people who had ever run for anything. I had run unsuccessfully for treasurer in 1976. Bob, my treasurer candidate had once been treasurer and also a candidate for mayor in the past. My third ward alderman had served one term as an alderman in the past. My city clerk was a lady I knew from my days in industry, but a local. My first ward alderman candidate had been a teacher and coach for many years and my second and fourth ward aldermen had never touched politics in any way shape or form. We were pretty much the blind leading the blind.

Our opponents were the Labor Party, the incumbents, and another Party of which I cannot remember their name. It was headed by a retired army sergeant from Herrin who was a big name in the American Legion. There were also a couple of independents also running for mayor. Moochie the current mayor was well loved in the community, but was already in his seventies. An older lady in my church told me she'd like to vote for me, but she owed it to vote for Moochie because his little grocery store had helped her during the depression. Besides, why did I want to get mixed up in that 'dirty' business?

Well, come election night the vote was counted but only a part of my slate won. My team got treasurer and wards one and four aldermen, so I didn't go into office with any big mandate, and I guess that is why the Progressive Party is not one of the big three parties today. We did turn out the largest vote in Herrin history however, and that still stands. Moochie was stunned because I beat him by 50 votes in over four thousand cast.

REGRETS, I'VE HAD A FEW

My guess is that if you've never had regrets, you haven't lived very long. You can learn good lessons or create a lot of memories from things that are regrettable, so sometimes it's a toss of a coin of what the wise move should have been.

For instance, in 1968 I moved my family to the community of Herrin, Illinois. This town of ten thousand residents is in Williamson County, Illinois, the subject of the book "Bloody Williamson." Herrin itself has its own history, but neither is a part of my regret. I went there as the controller of a major industrial plant with a work force of 1500. After about 4 years I left that job to start my own business because I didn't like the kind of life I was living and the politics involved in management. This isn't the regret that I'm referring to either.

I hung up my sign as a 'Certified Public Accountant' in Herrin hoping to attract enough business to house and feed my family. At that time, in the professional accounting world we were not allowed to advertise or solicit other accountants business. So, at the end of four years and our savings I thought it necessary to find a way to supplement my income. I looked for a stable income while maintaining my own business. The position of City Treasurer, a part-time position, didn't pay a lot but enough to tempt me to run for that office in 1976.

Herrin politics is non-partisan in the sense that major parties are not directly involved. Normally a group of seven persons will make up a ticket and call themselves by any name they chose such as Progressive, Labor, etc., running for the positions of Mayor, City Clerk, City Treasurer, and one person from each of the four Wards in Town. Historically you could find at least two such teams running at a given time but the votes were counted individually. The advantage of the team is that they could combine their finances and have the impact of working for each other. My problem was that I was a newcomer to town and no one knew me or asked me to be a part of their ticket, so I was left to run alone. I worked very hard at it canvassing 2000 of the 4000 residences in Herrin before time ran out. The local area newspaper endorsed one of the other candidates for the position. One was a retired postmaster and the other a local industry purchasing agent. They passed over the C.P.A., so my 800 votes came up short at election time.

Four years later I got my own team together for another try, this time as a candidate for Mayor. I was running against the incumbent mayor who was a beloved old gentleman that people called Moochie. Moochie had the distinction of being the first Italian Mayor in a community with a large Italian population. I had a good relationship with Moochie as I had served as City Auditor during his four years in office and wished him no ill will, but he just didn't have the energy to help the city at his advanced age. Another Italian put together a team to run and so we ended up with three complete slates and two independents running for the office of Mayor. I'm not sure this had ever happened before 1980 and I know it hasn't happened since. The odds of a newcomer in town beating 2 lifelong residents was pretty slim, but as it happened a record breaking vote turned out and I had 50 more votes than Moochie, and 700 more than the third candidate. Over 4300 ballots were cast in that election, and I won with 36 percent of the vote. Whether the Italian vote got split, or whether the other two candidates, non-Italians, votes made a difference we'll never know. Many were surprised.

I let it be known early that I was only there for four years as my accounting practice was growing and that was where I would need to put my future efforts. The Mayor position was not, nor did it pay like a full time position, but it helped. So when Ronald Reagan took his oath of office in January as President, I stepped up and took my oath for the office of Mayor in the first council meeting in May. I think the President had a longer honeymoon period that I did. By the first week in June we had had major town flooding, rioting on the strike line against the Teamsters at a local business, and a major tornado devastating a community ten mile away that involved our help for an extended period. The next two and a half years had many ups and downs, but when it came to the point that I could not lead because a major political party made it a point to take control of the aldermanic off season election, I decided to step down. This along with some personal reasons made me quit after serving only thirty-three of the forty-eight months I was elected for.

Regrets? Yes, I've had a few. In a way I regret ever getting into politics. I'm not one good at compromising. I had hate letters written to the local papers by a city workers wife because of the tough stand I made on negotiations with our public workers. I won't say I was always right, but I was always honest about what I was trying to do. I did not politic. My Dad died toward the end of my period in office. He had been so proud of me and he was always on the edge of politics himself. When he was gone, I lost some incentive. Yes, and I regret not having the fortitude to stick it out those last months. It's been 33 years now and that experience is long past, but the memories linger on.

HEIRLOOMS

One thing that I never had nor expected was heirlooms. I'll have to admit though that every once in a while I wished I had some remembrance from the distant past to look at and hold. The only thing that I had before two years ago was the family Bible that Mom and Dad bought in the middle forties to put the family names and birthdays down, hoping they would be forwarded on to the generations to come. I treasure that book, but I also protect it from the ravages of time. I wish I had something personal of my mother or my father. Dad bought me a hammer in 1978 and that is the best I can do.

Two years ago things changed for Marilyn and me. Her father died at the age of 105 years and from his estate she claimed a case built like an older china closet. That case has to be nearing 150 years old and it came from great grandfather Lycan who had it and used it as a medicine cabinet in his office as a doctor. It now sits in our office and holds many of our books and important items. It has a glass front and is still as sturdy as can be.

Among her father's belongings was an old cane that no one spoke for. It was offered to me, and I took it. It was a weird old cane in many respects with all kinds of carvings on it, but the wood was very beautiful. I put it in the closet and didn't think any more about it until a group that I belonged to needed a cane to fit the mood of the skit they performed. I dug it out and took it over and it worked. One of the older gentlemen really got interested in it and started thinking that I had a really old cane on my hands and maybe I should be careful how it was used. That perked my interest, and to make the story short I found a little information on the internet which led me to an appraiser that offered to look at it for me free of charge when I sent him a photograph. Just out my own curiosity I counted the individual carvings on the cane and they exceed 100 in number, with the largest being the head of the cane.

The appraiser's findings were that I had a Masonic Cane, probably carved in the Civil War era. He thought the value could possibly be $2500.00 in an auction of antiques or Masonic wares. It was a one of a kind and many of the symbols on the cane were masonic in nature, but there was about any type of animal native to America also carved on it. I was delighted to hear it and now I have my very own heirloom which I can pass on to my sons or daughter. Just in case that is not enough, I'll throw in a couple of my books. Will they qualify as heirlooms in a hundred and fifty years?

FROM THE PET PERSPECTIVE

By Sonny and Charlie Swinford

The name those people gave me was Sonny and I had no say in the matter. It's been about four years now and I don't know how they knew that I'd be so handsome and intelligent which to me is what sonny is all about. I've been laying here in this room that they provide for me since the first light of day and they still haven't come and opened my door so that I can eat and start my new day, which of course doesn't last all that long. Where are they? Have they already released that little chirper they call a dog? He can be such a pest. I'm the older and I should get priority and I normally do. Where are they?

I've been a wake for a while looking through the windowed door toward the center of the house. They can't get down the hall without me spotting them, but then they just keep going. I want to yell at them and say, 'hey your little Charlie wants out of this room, even as nice as it may be. I've been cooped up long enough.' I've been in his household now for just nine months now, but I've ruled it for the last five. Nothing happens without my attention. That cat in the other room may be bigger, but I stay awake longer and show much more affection than he does so that I get more attention. I can't take control though until they open these doors and let me out. Then everything is free game. Sonny's food, my food, their food, and the run of the house. Why do they call me Charlie? How should I know, ask them.

Well it's about time you opened my door big boy, where have you been? You used to be up with the dawn. Getting old? Yeh, that's right, put my bowls up on the counter so snoopy the dog can't get into them. Do we really need him here? Sure, I enjoy wrestling with him once in a while, but he never wants to stop. He thinks my ears are something for him to cut teeth on. He will finally stop when I give him the round house paw and a kick back with the rear paw. After that I normally get out the door for some privacy if the weather permits. There are birds and rabbits out there just hiding from me. Occasionally a friendly feline will stop by.

Why do you always feed that cat first and up on the counter to boot? You know you're going to relent sooner or later and let me have his left overs. He doesn't know how to clean his bowl like I do. For me it's good to the very last nublet. By the way, where is that other person who wears the prettier clothes and is nicer and soft to lay on? Isn't she ever going to get up? Why is her door still closed? Aren't you ever going to let her out to eat? You may feed me and let me sit on your lap and once in a while you'll comb my hair and bathe me, but in your heart you know I love her more. She's sweeter and she smells better. I just give you enough attention to keep you happy. I don't expect you to understand that.

How long I stay outside depends on the weather. In the winter I'll let them know that I want back in pretty quickly. I'll then eat some more, put up with Charlie for a while, take the high ground he can't reach for a nap, and then I decide when it's time for my daily rest. For that I get the master bedroom where I can have the door closed and have peace and quiet all day until dinner time. In the summertime I'll find a good napping spot out under the bushes. I like the heat. At dinner time I spend time with my family and the dog, and after a couple of hours outside I'm ready for my room for another night. A very tiresome day. Oh yes, and I'm much better groomed than that animal I live with. I spend hours cleaning myself. They have to give him a bath. Let them try that with me!

Except for a nap around mid-day, I keep busy. I like a lot of activity and in particular I love company to bark at and run in circles with. I'm an excellent paper shredder. Without my help, what would these people do if they didn't pick up after me? I love to lead the people around on a leash from time to time outside. One of our indoor games is to run and fetch. I like that game but sometimes the people are not very good. The pretty one is one lousy thrower. As often as not she sling the toy either under the couch or chairs, and expects me to get them out. It wasn't me that threw them under there. Let her get them out herself with that thing she always carries around and leans on. As for the big guy, he's a much better thrower, but he's also rougher. Can't he at least let me win a tug of war a time or two?

About seven in the evening after the cat has gone back outside I start settling down a little. I've entertained these people enough for one day. Sometimes they are watching something on the T.V. that I'll stare at from her lap for a while, but then it's time to stretch out on the floor until nine when I know the time is coming to get back in that room with the windowed doors. I really want to go to sleep, but I play hard to get until they put treats out on the floor for me and then I relent. They aren't all that smart.

Once in a while in a quiet time Charlie and Sonny will sit down and discuss the state of things. The topic is generally on how can we make things better here for ourselves. These people seem to want to please us. For old people they do pretty good but they sure are slow. They gave us names, maybe we should name them. What do you think of Felix and Spot? Are they the same sex? Well, if we don't know that, we sure can't name them.

WITH BUTTERFLY EARS

My wife and I have always loved animals, but when we moved back to town in 1994 we moved into an apartment and had to leave the animals behind. We had an empty nest with the children all gone, and no pets running around at our feet. That was before our landlord came up with the idea that they'd like us to move into one of their apartments under construction next door to their home. It would be a larger apartment and in a better neighborhood. In addition to that, we found out that they had a dog and they would allow us to have one too. The idea of having a brand new dwelling was very appealing and we decided to make the move.

We had a friend Anita that would occasionally need a sitter for her little dog and we gladly would help her out, sometimes for a week. It was a tiny little thing and a breed we had never heard of, a Papillion. (Pronounced Pap-e-on) The little girl weighed about eight pounds and had very large ears, the basis for the French name of Papillion having to do with butterfly wings. My wife fell in love with that little dog and I thought I would surprise her at Christmas by getting her one of her own. I located a pet store that could get one for me and was waiting for the day when they would call. Our friend Anita got wind of the fact that I was looking to buy a Papillion and mentioned that fact to my wife at church, not knowing it was to be a surprise. The Pet Store called the house when they had one and notified my wife when I wasn't there. So much for the surprise. She and I went to see if the newly weened puppy was acceptable and came home with an eight week old male weighing less than two pounds. He was a full blooded, papers to prove it breed, with a sire named Big Max and a momma named Paint. His markings were black and white and we named him Benji, Son of Big Max.

We lived on a corner of a street with very low traffic, and what traffic there was had to slow down to make the turn. Our yard connected with our neighbors offering a large area of grass uninterrupted in its spance. Although the town had leash ordinances, this never proved to be a problem for letting Benji have the run of the yards. It was ideal with only occasional corrections when he would want to get into the street as he thought he owned that also. The big plus side of outdoor living for him was that two of the neighbors also let their dogs out and he developed a friendship with Maggie and Ginger over the years. Both were older than he, but they got along great. Especially he and Maggie, the Landlord's little doggie.

Benji didn't stop in his growth when he reached twelve pounds, the usual size of a male Papillion. In fact, we had to watch his diet to make sure he didn't exceed twenty-five pounds too much. Now we understood the reason his sire was called Big Max. Regardless of size he turned out to be a wonderful companion for nearly twelve years. He rarely created any concerns for us, and when he did it was usually in the health realm. He was almost totally house broken from day one and loved to snuggle and snooze with both of his owners. He would travel with us on trips and loved people. He was a delight.

Later in his life he developed an enlarged liver and after about two years it erupted and in less than three days he was gone. The vets just couldn't come up with a solution for his problem. We were heartbroken but have sweet memories of our Benji. We got him a small memorial and buried him in our son's back yard, since we were still in an apartment at that time. We have a picture on the shelf in our office to remind us of him. We purchased another puppy about a year after losing Benji, largely because he left a hole in our lives. We love our new puppy Charlie, but we'll never forget our beautiful black and white doggy with butterfly ears that we called Benji, or just plain Ben.

WHERE HAVE ALL THE ANIMALS GONE?

Look around your neighborhood. Do you see anything? I don't, not even a stray cat or dog. You may hear a bark or two and there may be four footed creatures trotting around in your house, but their family.

Being brought up in a rural community I was used to seeing chickens, horses, cows and many other animals. Some were running loose and some weren't. I'm talking about inside the city limits, not just out in the country side. During the war the horse really got popular again when gasoline wasn't available. But that was years ago. Where have all the animals gone?

In 1968 I moved to Herrin, Illinois on East Stotlar Street. The Junior High School sat at one end of East Stotlar, and the Cemetery about marked the end of the street before it became a county road on the other end. I lived about half way in between and to my joy there was a small pasture with horses that I got to see every day. Also, you could also spot chickens and lots of stray dogs and cats. Stray dogs and cats could be nuisance, but seeing the horses was pure joy. They bothered no one. That was before the company I worked for decided it needed more land to expand and bought out the pasture and the horses disappeared. Today you can still see about three acres of asphalt parking lot where the horses used to run. It was the community's loss. The business is gone today also.

In 1984 the dirt in my veins won when I convinced my wife to move to the country. We found a house with 2 acres of land and I couldn't wait to get out there in the soil. My daughter loved horses and they were good therapy for her, so I immediately started construction on a small horse barn. A labor of love. When I had it almost finished she made it clear that she did not want a horse, she wanted to ride horses with other people around. This is what she had been doing for a while. At that point the barn became a very large dog house with a run and storage shed. I was a little disappointed, but we did have a beautiful black and white Collie mix to occupy the shed, and others to follow.

I didn't get my horse, but I got an unexpected bonus. A five foot wire fence separated me from the neighbors pasture, and he had at least six cows and a bull. We became acquainted and I fed them anything I could get my hands on and they kept coming back. The best time was when I could feed them the toppings from my garden produce which set right at the fence line. Then they would winter in another pasture and the farmer planted winter wheat. When that was harvested and the straw bailed, the cows would come back. That was a great season as the deers would come out of the woods with their new baby fauns. Every once in a while one would leap our fence and graze in our backyard. I loved to watch them. One year there was a twin fauns and I followed their growth for a while.

This went on for ten years until I needed to move back in town where ordinances had been passed and you don't see stray dogs and cats. You couldn't find one pullet in the city limit to fix a good meal, and the horses are lost in the country side. When's the last time you saw a Billy Goat? I miss them. Where have all the animals gone? Now all I have are memories of hearing of Old Nell, Star, Prince, and Butte. They may have pulled wagons and plows, but they were purebred memories to me.

NOT ONLY MAN'S BEST FRIEND

Our children grew up with pets. The first came to help our oldest to get over the fear of dogs. Frisky, named by our oldest, came to live with us when Brian was about 6. He did his job and became a dear friend of the family. He was only allowed into the house for visits as I didn't believe in house pets of the dog and cat nature. He was a black and white collie mix, being part Border Collie. He was well loved.

When our daughter came along she and her mother thought it was time for a nice house pet and I was out voted. We got a pedigree Poodle without the pedigree. Such a fancy dog deserved a special name, so it was agreed we would call him Maxwell after the Maxwell House Coffee box that housed his first bed. Now all were happy. The boys concentrated on Frisky and the girls on Maxwell. We soon shortened his name to Max.

Dogs being dogs, Frisky coming of age impregnated a little doggy that lived about a block and a half away, but spent all the time in our neighborhood and our yard. She loved our Frisky. I don't know how it happened but she gave birth to five or six puppies with long bodies and short legs. Really I do know how it happened as I was the one that had to get out the hose to get them separated. Anyway, we learned about the puppies when she brought some of them up under our bedroom window. We didn't quite know what to do so she housed them in the drain pipe running under our drive-way. It was a chore getting them out of there but we managed to get her family all safe, and because they were so cute the owners claimed them. They were unique. They came in every color, but their shape was all the same, a long body, big head and big ears. Poor Bandit, that was her name, she must have labored mightily. A Collie and a Pekinese mix. Frisky was so proud of them.

Dogs being dogs, Maxwell was not content to be put out on a leash on the patio and had a habit of trying to chew through the leash. On one Friday in late March of 1978, when Maxwell was about six years old, he got the job done and got his freedom. Kids were at school and Marilyn was busy with her daughter and the absence was not noted for a few hours. About midafternoon she realized that he was no longer there and went searching for him. She started calling, first me, then the neighbors, then the Radio Station, looking for a champaign colored Poodle dragging a partial leash. No luck. The boys and I scoured the neighborhood for hours without any luck. We had to give up and go to bed. The next morning we started all over again and were not successful. By noon we had one unhappy family, especially one little girl.

That evening the wife and I had a commitment to go out. The forecast was lousy and calling for snow. After dinner, just about dark, we were getting ready when Frisky started making a ruckus on the front porch. It took a while to realize that he wanted our attention. The boys and I in my evening going out wear decided to follow him. He went about a half block west and turned into a long drive and walked past the house into some weeds and brush that came up to our knees. There we found little Max entangled with the brush unable to dislodge himself. He was happy to see us and vice versa. We rushed him home to a very happy pair of females.

We went on to our card game that night and it had just started lightly snowing. By eight o'clock the next morning there was nineteen inches of snow on the ground paralyzing all of Southern Illinois. Maxwell was about ten inches tall. Frisky was not only 'man's best friend' but had saved his little buddies life.

NOSTALGIA

This whole week has been a nostalgic binge for me. Why? I'm not sure. Maybe that's what old people do, and yes I am an old person just completing the 79th. Celebration of my birth. What a fine day as I basked in well wishes and good food. I can honestly say, it is the best birthday I can recall in years.

Church, Family, Sunshine, and friends, how nice, but even tonight the nostalgia and days gone by are still there.

I currently live about 150 miles almost due south of the place of my birth, and my thoughts often go back to that time and that location. For years, one of the routes that I took to visit relatives in Paris came within 15 or 20 miles of the 'old home site', but I learned to fight the desire to take just one more trip down those old country roads. I knew when I yielded to temptation I was going to hear murmurs under my families breath of 'oh no, not again'. And I don't mean just the kids. For that reason, when another route became practical, I took it. That and the fact that I learned the old adage is true, "you can't go home again." You've all heard it.

As a young boy and man I always regretted not being able to go see the home of my Dad's childhood and the birth place of several of my siblings in Yellow Hammer. A couple of times Dad would take me down there when we would be mushrooming and show me where the house sat and the old well curb, but when I tried to find the place to show my wife and children in later years I couldn't even find the lane as trees and grass had taken over. For that reason, I made the trip to my old homesteads so the kids could find them to show to their kids, but as I said you can't go home again.

I learned that the kids weren't impressed when I would go down into the country and point to a place up on a bluff and tell them that was where I was actually born in Canaan School District. Of course there is nothing there except farm land now. It wasn't too far, so I'd cut across the country road to the old Bell School District and show them where I have my first memories from and where I lived when World War

171

II broke out. They were less than impressed again with the farm land where a house once stood.

I didn't want to bat zero with them so I headed for the small town of Oakland where I started to school and showed them the two story red brick house that I lived in for about a year. It's still standing and fairly impressive, so at least they had something to look at. Before leaving town and giving up on the tour, I also showed them the location where my fourth home had stood and how close to the downtown square that my 5th. home once was. Even I wasn't about to drive 60 miles to Decatur to show them where my 6th. home was once located. I'm smarter than that. You see, I learned the hard way that you can't go home again. Well almost.

Flash forward 20 years. It had become a ritual after Dad's death that my siblings and I would try to meet before Christmas for dinner and visiting. The idea was to find a spot that cut down on the travel for any one of us. One year someone got the idea to meet back in Oakland and stay in a bed and breakfast there overnight. It was a great idea. You guessed it, the Bed and Breakfast was the old Red Brick House of our youth. A couple had transformed it into a place of relative beauty, (in Oakland anyway) and the siblings who had traveled the furthest signed up to stay overnight and didn't have to worry about the weather etc. How nostalgic it was for the wife and I to have the exact bedroom of my youth. It had been sized down a little to accommodate more business, but it was real. I had come home for a while.

For a place that I only lived a year, it conjured up many memories. Imagine going from a 4 room farm house to an 11 room house in town. Thankfully, major improvement had been made to the old place. Now we had indoor plumbing, electricity, and indoor bathrooms. The layout was about as I remembered it. There were five bedrooms upstairs and six rooms downstairs. At the front of the house was the large parlor where my sister Hazel was married in 1942. That ceremony to a 5 year old probably wouldn't have made as much of an impact if the minister who married her had not been legless. He moved around on a board with wheels and could flip himself on and off chairs with ease. My parents loved that man.

Across the hall and back toward the middle of the house was a master bedroom with a big fireplace. That room stands out because on the day after Thanksgiving that same year, 1942, my sister Eula gave birth to Donna my niece. I remember when I was allowed in to see sis and the baby I was shown the box that Donna had come in. What a thrill. I always assumed that Donna had somehow been named after me because it was sister Eula who had named me. It was only in recent years that Donna told me that her mother told her that she was not named after me. Sis had wanted another name but her husband Louie had insisted on Donna. He may not have insisted had he known my sister named me after the cute boy over across the holler that she had taken a liking to when she was almost 13.

Another memory of the old house had changed. There was a small dinette off the kitchen which had a door leading outside. It almost had a small patio. When I first went to that area I was spooked by the stained glass window in the door. Who had stained glass windows in their door? Our church didn't even have stained glass windows. I grew accustomed in time and even appreciated having that handy door there to slip out and get a cup of fresh snow to make snow ice cream with. Breakfast around the big table in the dining area the next morning was very special.

Well, it's one thing to be nostalgic but I'll have to give it a rest. The old clock just pointed to twelve midnight which means my birthday is officially over. I need to go get some sleep and try to make it to the next one and appreciate the home I have now. (This was the first story I wrote this year that started an avalanche of short stories that led to this book.)

LOVE TRUMPS COMMON SENSE

Valentine's Day approaching brings many memories. I guess the theme of the day is love, although I doubt that is what kids think. They didn't seventy years ago. As I recall, my first valentines were paper cut-outs, probably introduced by our teachers. Then we progressed to the punch out types when the greeting card people saw a chance for making a dime. Then they became small one piece cards, normally with standups on them. By about the fifth grade it wasn't the type of card but the number of cards you received. Numbers equaled popularity. After that the exchange rate declined beginning in the early teens and became almost non-existent. That is until true love entered in the later teens when it took more than just a heart shaped card to show you really cared.

The day for me isn't about a card or a box of chocolates. It's all about the special meaning of Valentine's Day Eve sixty-two years ago. I was a junior in high school lacking many social skills and a little girl shy. A friend wanted to introduce me to a girl who used to be his neighbor. The opportunity finally arose at a basketball game on February 13, 1954. The girl he introduced me to with the light freckles, green eyes and heart shaped face completely blew me away. After the game others were going to a local hang out but I walked Marilyn home. She only lived three blocks away and I worked up the courage to ask her out. Whether it was for the next day, Valentine's Day, or not I can't be sure but that heart shaped face made a lasting impression.

My dad always professed common sense over intelligence. People can be genius, but without common sense they can be useless. Common sense is a very important element in our lives.

Some two years plus later I was stationed at Fort Devens, Massachusetts, an Army post near Boston. I was in schooling preparing for overseas duty to fill my military obligation. In March I found out that I'd be going to the Far East the first week of April. This meant that I would not be home again for 15 to 16 more months, making it a full year and a half away from home. In late March we were given a three day pass with restrictions allowing us to travel no more than 200 miles. Common sense told me that there was no way I should try to make it 1000 miles to Illinois, but the thought of seeing that gal with the heart shaped face, lightly freckled, with green eyes made me buy a round trip plane ticket home. I'd fly into Indianapolis where my dad would pick me up and be home to Paris by Friday evening. On Sunday my brother Cleo and his wife would drive me back to Indianapolis for my return flight. I wouldn't have much more than 36 hours with my family and Marilyn, my sweetheart by this time, but I couldn't leave without seeing her. We made the tough decisions like she should date when she went to college and all of that, but our undying pledge was to one another. The trip was worth it. Love trumped common sense.

Everything was on schedule as my brother took me to Indianapolis. One fly in the ointment was that the east was having big snow storms and we learned at the Airport that some flights were being cancelled. Even worse, we had missed my plane. Although Indianapolis is only ninety miles east of Paris, Illinois, they are in the Eastern Time zone, a fact we had forgotten. What was confusing was the fact that back in the fifties; Terre Haute, Indiana was in the Central Time Zone also. Regardless, the scramble was on. I had about 900 miles to cover and about 15 hours to reveille when role call would be taken. I finally made a connection from Indianapolis to Cleveland where I could catch a plane to Pittsburg where I could catch a plane to New York City, where I could catch a plane to Boston. At two a.m. I was in the terminal in New York City awaiting notice of whether the Boston Airport had been opened yet after receiving almost two feet of snow. I was on the first plane out. There weren't too many passengers on my flight. It had been an expensive journey and I found that the food in Airports is not cheap. When I arrived in Boston I had five dollars to my name and the need of a taxi to take me 35 miles to the post. Who would think that with the snow packed roads that a cab driver would consider taking a foolish young man over those roads and accept a check on an Illinois bank? Thank God, I only wished I had gotten his name and address. I was beside my bunk at 20 minutes to reveille.

I've never claimed to be a genius, and this story I'm telling on myself speaks to common sense, but it tells that in a given situation that love trumps common sense. I'm glad it did. Valentine's Day eve will mark our sixty-two years knowing each other, and guess what, the beautiful gal with the heart shaped face and green eyes is in the next room. The freckles have disappeared however, except for the arms, but I've always loved them also.

PUNISHABLE CRIME?

Laws are made to protect society, or that is what they are supposed to do. In the Military they have their own code of justice. An Article Nine might get you an eight hour punishment of picking up cigarette butts. Then there are Court Martials where the military brass determines if the crime committed is worthy of stockade time or giving an individual the old heave ho out of the service. Then there is Treason. The unforgiveable crime that is possibly punishable by death. They have this in the civil law also. In war time it could be a firing squad.

This is not a complete listing of crime and punishment, but is shown for just one reason. When a person enlists or is drafted into the service of this nation, they are sworn to defend and may pay for it with their lives. For this they should be given the utmost respect by our citizens and be backed to the hilt. The people they are protecting should not belittle or cause them unnecessary pain of any kind. The government expects the most of the soldier, sailor, marine, coast guard, or air force men and women, and in return they should always have their back.

An illustration. Suppose a young man nineteen years of age was doing his duty in Korea in 1956. And although it was peacetime, if he had gone over to the enemy and given up secrets he could be charged with treason. All of the shame would be put upon his family and he might never return home.

On the other hand, suppose that clean living young G.I. was faithfully writing his darling back home every day and repeatedly telling her he couldn't wait to get back and make a life with her forever, He was also daily doing what he was trained to do to help protect everyone back home, and then one day the letter comes. It looked just like any other letter and was addressed to him at this A.P.O. number and had probably been in route for a week to ten days. He couldn't wait to find privacy to open it. When he did, he stopped short, and looked at the envelope again. Yes, it was addressed to him, so why did the greeting start out Dear John, instead of Hello Darling. His name wasn't John. As he read on the wind went out of his sails. It was to him and the meaning became very clear. She did not plan to wait on the guy working to defend her to death in Korea.

You can only imagine the affect this had on this bright young man with a spotless record who had made a total commitment to this young lady for life. Maybe it wasn't treason in the Army sense, but it was a close second. Shouldn't someone rise up and see that justice was served.

In the following days he would get up hoping that the dark clouds had lifted some, but it was just the drudgery of breakfast and another day of defending the American way, even if he wasn't respected. The buddies that he ashamedly shared his bad news with were one hundred per cent on his side and shared his anger that no one had risen to his defense. It could have been them. During those evenings demon rum may have even crossed his mind a time or two, he didn't know if he could ever rebound. But just in time another letter came. She took it all back.

He forgave her. She didn't say go into any detail about why she had done what she did, but he suspected that she was going through hell week in her freshman year of college and had to do something like this in order to get into a sorority or something. For that he never cared much for Greek Houses.

Let's just say that in the hypothetical story that someone could have set a standard making it a very serious deal and there would be very few Dear Johns. It didn't necessarily have to be a death sentence.

AFFORDABLE HOUSING

After WWII when tens of thousands of men and women were returning from the conflict, Colleges and Universities had a need of building projects to offer these potential students homes. Many were married with families and affordability was essential. Most would be attending under the G.I. Bill benefit program. They had to be built quickly, and they had to be affordable.

At the University of Illinois this housing took two basic forms at two locations. On the Champaign side next to the Memorial Football field would be the traditional duplex type of unit that would house two families. They were sturdy and had siding and some porches. On the Urbana side was the basic necessity unit constructed of 3/4th. inch plywood. They had one front door and came in two sizes, one bedroom and two bedrooms. These were located in the southern most campus, almost as if they were to be kept out of sight.

The one bedroom unit had approximately 300 square foot of space which is about the size of a decent living room in modern housing. It provided a coke burning stove, a sink, a hot plate, some cupboards, a refrigerator, a hot water heater, and a shower and stool. It did have a hookup for a washer that could drain in the stool for anyone who could afford one, and provided clothes line poles in the rear yard. One set of windows would open on a spring and chain system and could be covered with plastic in the winter to keep out the winds.

Why would anyone choose to live like this? Number one, chances are that the G.I.'s had been living in much worse conditions for a long time. Secondly, all of these benefits cost less than thirty dollars. In 1958 the price had risen to forty three dollars. You had to provide your own telephone and television, otherwise it was one price paid all. A one bedroom arrangement in the community would cost double so this is why so many men and women benefitted from the efforts made to accommodate them.

As a veteran of the peace time Army I was eligible for this housing even though I was not eligible for the G.I. Bill. These units made the difference for me completing my studies and moving on and I'm grateful for that. For two of these units, the wife and I were the last occupants before they were demolished. After about a year in the first house the University moved us into a second house in order to start their new building program. Upon graduation, the second unit was never used again as all were torn down to make way for modern dormitories.

When I look around at the slums and homeless of today, I wonder why we can't have more affordable housing. I know programs of this nature failed miserably in the cities, but why? What's the excuse in small towns where the need exist and churches do it on a small scale without the government. Couldn't we all do better to help our neighbors?

THE SHELTER

If there was one thing I learned about my wife early on in our marriage, it was the fact that she did not like storms. This was highlighted when we were living in our first house on the campus at the University. They were made out of plywood for returning veterans and were about the size of a trailer and not particularly storm resistant. The University had given us instructions on what to do in case of tornado warning. My wife pinned it to the wall and memorized it the first day. They stated in so many words that our shelter was the basement of the fraternity house fifty yards in front of our unit. I don't know why she worried. During the day time she was generally in class and at night I was working. Maybe that was the problem. Anyway, we survived with only having to take that shelter one time in three years.

Later we were living in an apartment in Chicago at the time of the Bay of Pigs incident when Cuba was invaded by troops supported by the U.S. After the Russians moved into Cuba and started building missile sites my wife started looking for shelters. The news said they would have the capability of launching a missile that could strike Chicago and that was enough for her. We came from downstate Illinois and they could have Chicago, but not while we were there. It was then that I came home one day to find she had located a shelter in the next apartment building basement for us. She wanted to be ready.

After Chicago, we lived in Rockford two years and we felt safer about missile strikes. Back then the tornados tended to stay further south and I don't think we ever experienced one in Rockford. She was ready if we did though. Our apartment had a full basement and we didn't even have to exit the building to get there. We were secure. She was left home alone quite a lot and I'm sure when the clouds darkened she found an excuse to do laundry in the basement.

Then we moved to tornado alley in Southern Illinois with a history of some dandies. Facts bore out that this strip of land from South East Missouri to Indiana could be hazardous to one's health. I was a believer but always felt if it was my time it would find me anyway. Our first home in Herrin had a full basement and Marilyn made good use to it. By then we had a growing family and she was going to shelter them through thick and thin, and if it clouded up they went to the basement. More times than once I came home to find my family huddled in the south west corner of our basement sitting on padded mattresses with blankets and the radio. Normally after a little coaxing and the assurance that the dark clouds were lifting, she would allow everyone back upstairs.

She never missed an alert. The city even had sirens they set off. Of course if the wind was in the wrong direction you could barely hear them if you were listening. One Saturday morning we were still at the kitchen table having a second cup of coffee when I noted tin foil floating through the air. There were lots of small pieces and they just kept floating by and I pointed them out to the wife. The sky was light and sun was reflecting off of the foil and we watched in wonderment. It was only later when she turned on the radio that we discovered Herrin had been hit by a tornado less than a mile from the house. In fact the street that ran in front of our house was closed due to downed power lines and tree limbs. I'm not sure but I think I heard her give a big gulp. I do know that even though serious storms and tornados still come to Southern Illinois, my wife is less apt to panic. Let's just say that she no longer over reacts. However, we moved a year or so ago and I'm sure she has secretly picked out the safest spot in our new home, just in case. In fact I just took time to question her and got a prompt answer to that question and now I know where I can go. Don't take that the wrong way....

OUR DAY IN COURT

If you've never been there, a Court Room can be a pretty intimidating place for a person. The wife and I had always tried to be law abiding citizens and obeyed the laws of our land. I had even served three years in the military and had the highest respect for authority. I think my civics teacher in high school imbedded much of this in me as we studied the constitution and how laws were made and enforced. My folks had taught me the practical things, but an understanding of how things worked came from the education I received.

I remember one of my favorite T.V. shows at the time was Perry Mason. Other than the fact that the guy who played Perry was first a bad guy in the B Westerns of my youth, I watched many of court scenes with all the drama that went on. I had a fascination with it. I did have a run in with the law as a teenager, but going before the Justice of Peace in his home and paying a sixteen dollar fine wasn't the same.

Life started off normally that March morning in 1966 when I got up and went to my job in Olney, Illinois. Things were going along pretty smoothly on my job; I had only been there for about seven months. That day, in the late afternoon I got a call from my wife telling me the sheriff had just been there and left a subpoena. We were to show up in court at a given time and advised to get an attorney. We didn't hesitate to do the latter. We knew we'd have some legal work someday, but the way this came about kind of shocked us.

The Court House in Richland County Illinois was an old two storied structure on the main street in Olney. It wasn't particularly impressive, but the outside looked better than the interior which was really run down. We met our attorney and he led us around to a rather large courtroom with old fashioned chairs and tables. He explained to us that our case would not involve any kind of jury, but would be a bench trial. He would have to put my wife on the stand and ask her some leading questions before she would be cross examined by the attorney for the defendant. We took his word for it that this would be the best way to handle it.

The Judge and other court personnel came in and the Judge called the court to order. I don't remember whether there was a pledge to the flag or not. I was too nervous. Our case was called and the attorneys introduced themselves and their clients. Without any delay my wife was called to testify. She was asked detailed questions about her personal life and our home. The attorney led her gently through the process and she did a good job. When he finished the attorney for the defendant took over and grilled her on her answers seeing if she would change any of her answers. He was very impersonal and it seemed the questioning was much longer and intense that what was necessary. Finally he finished.

I was called next, and after a few personal questions about my job and my life I was turned over to be cross examined. I gripped the arm of my chair as the attorney approached me. I had been sworn in and knew I'd have to be fully honest in anything I told him, and I didn't want to mess up. His opening statement to me was, 'if I asked you the same questions regarding your married life and home as I asked your wife, would you give me the same answers'? I'm sure I hesitated slightly to understand what he was asking, but then assured him that I would. He then told the Judge, 'no further questions' and the Judge excused me. What now I wondered?

The Judge then said that if there were no further witnesses, he was ready to make a decision in the case. Both attorneys said they were finished and the Judge proceeded. Fortunately he concluded that the wife and I should thereafter be the legally adopted parents of one Brian James Swinford. Any and all rights of parenthood were now ours and no one could challenge that fact. Our son, ten months old at that time and having been in our home since he was two months old, would forever more be ours. All we had to do after that was pay our attorney and also the defendant's attorney's fee. I don't guess there's any conflict of interest there.

THAT HELPLESS FEELING

I'm no expert. I've only had the experience of sitting in a maternity ward waiting room two times when my wife was in the delivery room, but does it get any easier with numbers? My dad never talked to me about this part of life even though he and my mother had eight children. Of course, all of them were born at home. No waiting room there. I suppose by the time I came along my dad didn't even bother to come in out of the fields. My point here is that there is no training for the big event.

My first experience was with my middle child Bill. That's right, just plain Bill, short for William. I put that moniker on him and have never lived it down. His grandmother who was lobbying for Charles never let me live it down, and Bill never liked his name. What's not to like? A perfectly good wholesome name. My wife has kept her peace because she got to name our first son and it was my turn. Incidentally, she named our third child too and then quit on me. Two to one, that's not fair.

August 19, 1966 started off as a routine day. My wife was having a backache but It was a workday so I got up and had breakfast and went to work. My place of employment was only about two miles south of the house, so it isn't as though I'd be out of touch. As I recall I even went home for lunch and

Marilyn, my wife, wasn't feeling that great and wasn't sure what was happening. The doctors had placed her due date around the first week of September. I know more than got back to work when the phone rang and I was wanted at home. It didn't take me long to get there, but when I did there was no panic. She had gone into labor but we appeared to have a lot of time. We even called the in-laws as the plan was they'd come down and take our fifteen month old son Brian home with them to Paris, Illinois, eighty five miles north. They would keep him while his mother was in the hospital. In the interim a sitter would stay with him.

We loaded into the car and headed for the Richland County Hospital which was just on the other side of town in Olney, Illinois, the home of the White Squirrels. Her doctor had been notified. By this time it was about four p.m. Marilyn was increasingly uncomfortable but they let me stay with her until about five thirty when they kicked me out of the holding room. Unlike some hospitals Richland County did not have a maternity waiting room. The one waiting room for everyone was the lobby. That's where I ended up pacing the floor. Yes it's true, this new father to be did pace.

I don't recall there being any coke or soda machines. If there were candy or sandwich machines, I don't recall them. i can't imagine me going through the dinner hour without something though. For the better part of two hours I made the rounds in the lobby of the hospital without a word of what was going on. I didn't know the score. I didn't know the etiquette? Was there a loud speaker or flashing lights or dancing nurses? No one told me how long it would take nor did I ever see the doctor. I ended up standing with my head hanging out into the hospital hallway looking around. Finally a nurse who looked vaguely familiar passed and I asked her about my wife. She looked at me and said my wife was in her room. Wasn't I told? I had a baby boy born about an hour and a half ago. By the time I found her room I didn't know what to say to her about not being there for her. I didn't need to say anything. They had her so drugged that she didn't really care.

My memory is that I didn't get to see Bill until the next morning because he was jaundice and was having Bilirubin Test. Marilyn was breast feeding so she got to see him regularly. Back then they kept mom and babies for at least three days and by the time I got them home our son Brian didn't want anything to do with a mother who would desert him for whatever that was in her arms. He didn't want anything to do with Bill for a while either, but he got over it. Bill's grandparents were there to greet him when he got home along with his Aunt Kathie. All went well until his Aunt Kathi said she thought he looked like Porky the Pig. We're still trying to get over that one. So what if it took a while before his beauty and charm came through. More importantly, I had survived my first deliverance.

TWO MONTHS EARLY

We were living with our two boys on Stotlar Street in Herrin, Illinois that first week in November, 1969. It was a Wednesday and the wife had cleaned the oven that day and was talking on the phone with a friend after dinner. When she called my name from the kitchen it sounded a little frantic. She was nearly seven months pregnant and her water had broken.

We weren't prepared for this but acted as quickly as we could. A call to the doctor instructed us to come to the hospital. A call to a friend got us a sitter for our boys and then my wife got in the back seat of the car. We headed for Carbondale, my wife wrapped in the coat I had gotten her for Christmas, and in the glistening rain I prayed all the way for God to watch over her. The coat was disposed of after the trip.

The Holden Hospital in Carbondale was less than twenty miles away. It was an old hospital that was being replaced by a newer one and being phased out, but was still the one used for deliveries. We had never been there before. The staff took over in the emergency room and I sat down and waited. Looking around it was clear that there had been no maintenance on the building in a long time. Walls were stained and cracks appeared everywhere. Unknown to me then, it would close its doors just months later and be torn down. Finally someone came and told me that my wife was resting. She was not in labor but because her water had broken the doctor wanted her in the hospital on bed rest. It was just a matter of time before she would go into labor. I was told to go home and get some rest.

The next two days was more of the same, and sometime along the way my wife's mother came down from Central Illinois to help with the boys and encourage her daughter. Basically there was no change and sitting by her bed side to keep her company was all we could do.

On Saturday things started to change. The Doctor had stopped by in the morning and told my wife not to deliver during the ball game in the afternoon. Southern Illinois University had a football game that afternoon and he would be there. By noon my mother-in-law and I were run out of the room by the nurses and confined to the waiting room, which like the rest of the hospital was pitiful. As we sat there together the question of names came up. When our second son was born my wife's mother had lobbied for the name Charles, after her father. She was disappointed I'm sure when we named him William after no one in particular. The wife let me pick the name as she had named our oldest son Brian. For some reason I always wanted a son named 'just plain Bill'. When I told her our choice for a little girls name I thought she would hit the ceiling. Her name was Helen and when I told her Marilyn had chosen the name Beth Ellen, she thought I was saying Beth Helen. I know it was a letdown when I had to spell out the difference, but she didn't let on.

That's where we were at three fifteen in the afternoon when a doctor came to the waiting room and told me that I had a baby daughter and that she and my wife were doing okay. We first were allowed to go and look at Beth through a window and then a while later we got to visit Marilyn in her room. Beth looked so much like a beautiful doll with lots of black hair. We learned that she weighed in at three pounds eight ounces and was nineteen inches long. We also learned that it was policy that all premature babies were sent to a special hospital in East St. Louis for care until they had reached at least five pounds. This was disappointing to find out that we couldn't have her with us, but were assured it was best for the baby. We could call there at any time and get a report on her. After the delivery, Marilyn only got to see Beth one-time before the transfer. They brought Beth to the room in an incubator.

The transfer to East St. Louis was made in the wee hours of Sunday morning. My wife remained in the hospital until Monday morning. It was on Monday that we placed our first phone call to found out about our daughter. We were told that she had developed breathing problems and had turned blue, but she was stable at this point. My wife couldn't travel but it was decided that I would make the trip up on a Thursday to see for myself what was going on. When I got to the hospital I was allowed to see Beth in an incubator hooked up with tubes. She had lost eight ounces which was 1/7th of her body weight, and she looked entirely different than when I had seen her earlier. She looked very wrinkled and poor. I was heartbroken. The nurses said she was responding and things would get better. There were no other details available. All we know is that sometime between the early Sunday morning hours and Monday morning, our daughter had breathing problems.

A month later we got our daughter home. She had gained to four pound and ten ounces and was looking good once again and the medical staff decided it was safe to release her before she got to five pounds. It would be almost thirteen years before we'd release her to someone else's care even for a little while. She was and is our special child.

Things that didn't happen right in those few days in November 1969 were that Marilyn's Obstetrician didn't show up for the delivery. He was at the football game on the other side of campus and the doctor on duty delivered our daughter after the nurses had already started. Another thing was, when all the insurance papers cleared with my company insurance plan, there was no ambulance taking our daughter on that two hour trip. A car had been used. Could that have been when she developed difficulties and didn't have the proper equipment to help?

Two things that happened right that November was my wife came through it all just fine, and secondly we have the most precious gift of all. She has gone on to get a degree in Social Work and marry the love of her life Lee Smith, who like her had faced life's challenges. He was taken from her after less than a year's marriage but his sweet memories live on in her heart and the heart of her family. She continues to live an independent life in her own home, making the most of each day.

MELODY OF LOVE

We've all had life changing events. One of mine was the birth of our daughter in November of 1969. She was premature, and it was taking her time to catch up weight wise and overall size. Her physical development was a little slow but that was due to the early start, we thought. It was November 1970 before the doctors told us that our daughter had Cerebral Palsy. This was caused by the lack of oxygen sometime before or after her birth that caused damage to her brain. The extent would only be known with time. The following year she responded very well in every way except her legs and right arm. She was bright; she was cheerful and very social. Her eyes and hearing were not affected. The prognosis was a lifetime of physical therapy just to maximize what she could do physically, and that she may or may not ever walk without assistance.

In 1972 I went into business for myself and found a lot of idle time on my hands, so I had time to spend with all my children. At the office I found myself writing lyrics about my special child. At home I found myself playing my guitar more and putting the lyrics to music to sing to my daughter. I was not an accomplished player, but it just took a few simple chords to put together the song. It turned out to have three verses and a chorus that I would sing to her. I named the song "Special Child" and the first verse and chorus went like this:

Why it happened no one can say

But heaven opened its door one day

And sent her down, for me to love.

She seemed oh so very bright

A perfect bundle of delight

But in a while, I knew God had sent

A Special Child.

(chorus)

Oh the smile on her face, contains heavens grace

And the light in her eyes like the stars.

She's my heaven on earth, since the day of her birth

And I know God has sent me a Special Child.

That year I heard they were having auditions for a Cerebral Palsy telethon to be held at the CBS affiliate in Cape Girardeau, Missouri. The auditions were being held on the campus of Southern Illinois University in Carbondale, Illinois. With time on my hands the wife and I took our daughter and my guitar and went over and I sang my song while the wife held our daughter. She was beautiful and we were very proud of her and it was something I wanted to do. Out of many applicants just in Southern Illinois we were one of the handful selected to appear on the live broadcast hosted by Johnny Tillitson who at that time was having considerable success nationally.

The telethon actually lasted all day starting at about 8 a.m. on a Sunday morning. We were told to be there around 1 p.m. in the afternoon and that the telethon would conclude at about 5 p.m. It was about a sixty five mile drive and we took the boys, aged 6 and 7 at that time, and left for our adventure. They were thrilled at meeting Ronald McDonald and we all watched the telethon in a waiting room. At about 3:30 p.m. we were taken to the actual set and arranged for our song. The boys were positioned on the bleachers nearby to watch. We were advised on how to address the camera and how we would be introduced. The announcer gave us our cue and while my wife held our daughter in her beautiful long dress, both looking at me, I played and sang her song. I don't know why, but I didn't choke or freeze up. I was cool and calm. After I sang, Johnny Tillitson came over and interviewed us for the audience. We then got in our car and came home. I had several people tell me that they were sure that the final rush of donations to the cause was a result of our appearance. I like to think we helped.

Twenty years later my daughter was a social worker having graduated from S.I.U. and working for a group supporting people with disabilities. As a para-pelagic herself, she could relate very well to people and had become a spokesman for her organization. As such, the local affiliate for A.B.C. called on her to help as an announcer in a Telethon for Cerebral Palsy which she was happy to do. They found out about our earlier adventure years before and wanted to use the song for the telethon. By that time I had a friend re-write the music for my lyrics and record it for me. They used that recording numerous times during the telethon. By her work and her independence she has illustrated to the world that she is indeed very special.

She's always made me feel that the number is special to her. I have no answer for my young sons when they asked why I didn't write one about them. Now in maturity I know they understand the why of that one. Her song just came to me as a 'melody of love'.

STOTLAR STREET

Taking a new job in 1968 meant having to find a house suitable for my pocketbook and my family, in that order. A local realtor showed us around and we found a nice three bedroom house with a full basement and one and a half baths. This appeared ideal for our family consisting of a 3 year old and a 2 year old at the time, so in August 1968 we moved in. The house was situated on a street that served as a secondary highway off of routes 37 and 55. When people came off of the interstate and wanted to by-pass the downtown area, they could come in on Stotlar Street. It wasn't heavy traffic, but also trucks hauling materials in and out of the Norge Plant where I worked used that road.

We truly enjoyed the home and ended up finishing off part of the basement where we had a family room and a play room for the boys. The backyard was great for outdoor toys and room to romp. The lot was 75X150 feet with just the right kind of scrubs, trees, and bushes to give us some privacy. It was more space than we had ever had.

Everything went along quite nicely, and then along came a daughter in November of 1969. Now the stairs became a little problem when it came to transporting our baby up and down some rather narrow stairways. We managed it, but it wasn't ideal. As she grew older she would want to be where the boys were and we could not trust the small boys to look out for her. She needed special attention sometimes. The living room upstairs began to get more use and the Television made its way back upstairs, or maybe it was a duplicate.

The boys in 1971 were five and six respectively and very active in the backyard. They met other neighbor boys from adjoining lawns and it was a great place to play. Plastic swimming pools and tree houses were very popular. They both had pedal cars that they shared. One a sedan and one a bright red fire truck with ladders. In addition there was a wagon and a bicycle with training wheels.

We watched over them pretty closely as we had a habit of being over protective. They were checked from time to time. One afternoon, it must have been a Saturday; I was washing the car in the driveway. Traffic was normally less as people were not going to work as much and traffic to the plant was minimal. It was then that I heard a voice from some distance away saying 'hi dad'. I turned to see my youngest son in his sedan pedal car coming down Stotlar Street from Fourth Street. My heart fell in my chest. Don't get me wrong, he was driving on the right side of the road and all, but he was traveling way below the posted speed limit. I moved a lot faster getting to him and getting him off the shoulder of the road into the neighbors grass. I don't remember whether there was any cars coming or not, but I hoped my neighbors had not seen this. I'm sure it never happened to them.

It wasn't long after that when a house came available just three blocks north of where we lived on a dead end street. Friends of ours had taken a new job and we were familiar with the house and the decision was made to leave Stotlar Street. That is how and why we became residents of Pine Street in Herrin, Illinois.

THE ADVENTURER

The wife and I were alike when it came to raising our children. We tended to keep them on a short leash and like us they were not overly adventurous, which was fine with us. Like any parents we enjoyed our time in the city park with the slides, swings, and other things that we could keep our eyes on and cautioned them where necessary. As a result of over protectiveness, they were not quick to try new things.

Our daughter had a more adventurous spirit, but she had not come along when the Swinford family decided their hand at camping. This was a new adventure for the two little boys, and new trials for the parents. I had not camped since my army days and my wife had not done much since she was an active girl scout.

We started from scratch. We went to the discount store and surplus store to locate a tent, lanterns, and all that was necessary to live in the wilds. The blue and yellow plastic tent wasn't what I was really looking for, but was the only one we could afford. It would have to do. It came in a plastic sack complete with poles and plastic anchor pens.

Living on the edge of a National Forest, there had to be many spots to go camping that didn't have bears or snakes. Talking around with people who had been in this area all their lives or a number of years, we settled on Pound Hollow which was about thirty five miles away and had a nice camping area and a stream running through. So one Friday after work we loaded the car and with our three and four year old boys set out in very good spirits for a new adventure.

Pound Hollow sits on the southeastern part of the state, and I don't even know if it's considered a part of the Shawnee National Forest but it was good enough for us. We drove around to see what was available and there was hardly anyone there. It was fairly large and the stream running through it appeared clean and inviting. The spot we found was a level or two above the stream and the site big enough for our tent, table, and car. There were no other tents in sight, but being a Friday evening we assumed the place would fill up before the weekend was over. Who wouldn't want to camp there?

We unloaded the car, got the boys situated, and selected the spot for our tent. We soon wished that we had done a dry run on the tent as we were having trouble figuring it out. The thing didn't come with instructions and we were busy trying to figure out what was front and back and how the poles went. In the process we neglected to keep a close eye on the boys. It never crossed our mind that they would venture off, they never had. Things only got worse when it started raining and we panicked. Fortunately a Park Ranger stopped by at that time and helped us to figure out the tent. When he had helped us and moved on we were getting things in out of the rain and the boys were not in the car where we had left them. They were not in the camp site.

Behind our camping area the land sloped down through the trees toward the road below. You couldn't see very far through the trees so we called their names and walked down the hill. When they didn't respond I decided to go down the road while my wife stayed at the camp and continued calling their names. I got into the car and started down the road that descended to the stream below. As I came around the curve in the road there were the boys marching up the middle of the road. One was aggressively leading and the other crying for all his worth. You can believe that a quick prayer of thanks went up just then. Brian, the older, was not fazed, but Bill did not share his confidence or love of the great outdoors at that time.

Lesson learned. While we taught our children to be cautious and by nature not very adventurous, that did not apply to Brian when it came to natures forests and trees. He had found his element and would thereafter explore the great outdoors whenever and wherever he could. It would be a few years before he got over the fear of dogs and other things, but that didn't apply to exploration of the great unknowns. He has always been drawn to the rocks and the trees and if my memory serves me correct, I believe that is where he took his future wife to propose to her.

PERILOUS TIMES

Water is a necessity of life. You've got to love it but it also offers perils. The people in Noah's day found that out too late. Through the centuries the waters have created havoc. So, the water giveth and the water taketh away.

As a kid I truly tried to learn to swim. I could dog paddle a few feet but had no endurance. I just wasn't buoyant. I worked on all the fundamentals on the overhand stroke, but when I turned my head to the side to catch a breathe all I got was water. That, and being scared by some near misses in my youth, I never developed a love for the water as a recreational endeavor.

For this reason, I can only recall one time as a kid going out in a rowboat. My older brother-in-law wanted me to go fishing with him at the local lake. He rented a boat and we went out to the middle of the lake to fish. I was very uneasy but tried not to show him that I was a coward. Besides, I had never fished from a boat. He loaned me a rod and reel that I also had never used. We had always used cane poles from the shores. Harold demonstrated the use of the rod and reel and stressed how you triggered the reel. I got my hook baited and made my first mighty cast. I forgot one small detail. I forgot to properly use the reel and got a whiplash. The embarrassment I had for the next two hours trying to untangle that line almost made me forget that I was on the water. That was the last time I ever fished out of a row boat.

Now you know why I never joined the Navy although my brother Aaron and best friend Luther did. Luther could swim about as well as me. I'm surprised he survived. At least the Army stayed on good old terra ferma, except when they were shipping us someplace of course.

The next boat ride for me was a little different and in my Army days. In April of 1956 I stepped foot on the biggest boat I had ever seen in person. It was named after some Admiral of somebody important and carried a couple of thousand troops. It embarked from Seattle for Yokahoma, Japan on a ten day cruise. For some unknown reason they took what they called the northern route, meaning it was colder in April on the high seas, and the waves were rougher. The accommodations were not great as the bunks only allowed eighteen inches between you and the guy above you, but during the day you couldn't just lounge in them anyway. Most of the time you were up on deck in daylight hours because there would always be a lot of cleaning going on below and you had to be out.

I think l would have been just fine with the rough seas and cold winds had half of the G.I.s aboard not have had troubles. When one person would get sea sick in the compartments or stairwells that would trigger the biggest messes imaginable and that is what you had to face heading for the open air and rail. Enough of that story. I'll just conclude that I most likely lost weight on that ten day cruise. Fortunately in Japan we regrouped and went on by plane to Korea. The return trip 15 months later from Korea had other perils.

The lady I married loves the water. She'd swim every day if she could. A moonlight paddle in the boat would probably have been to her liking, but she could care less about fishing over the side of a row boat. With me, she got neither. There was no cruising down the river on a Sunday Afternoon with me.

This was true until years later when we visited her folks camped near the Kentucky Lake. By then we had two sons aged four and three. With rental boats everywhere they wanted to go out on the water like the other kids did. How do you tell your boys that you're a coward and can't go, so I rented a boat. The wife two boys and I set out in a small boat with a small motor, having paid for a two hour excursion. The boys were loving it and didn't particularly notice that we were never more that 50 to 75 feet from the shoreline. At one point the shoreline turned left out toward the more open water. We were still in close proximity to land so we followed on out on the peninsula. Everyone was enjoying the nice slow smooth ride when the wife noticed the time. To reverse our trail would take much too long to get back to the dock, so we would have to cross over open water to get back in time. This meant the waves would come towards the side of the boat and we'd need to go a little faster. The ride got much rougher. With every one holding tight I did the best I could to fight the waves, but had zero experience. Did I mention that the swimmer of our family was my wife? Did I mention that she was about 5 months pregnant? That crossing probably was less than 200 yards, but it took forever and I swore that would never happen again. The kids still wanted to go on the water on the smaller lakes after that and we did. We'd go on pontoon boats and little paddle wheelers. We were even part owner of a sixteen foot cruiser one time that I couldn't keep running. I rarely got it out of the harbor on a lake we used that must have been almost six foot deep in most places.

PROUD MOMENTS THAT LAST A LIFE TIME

They say that pride comes before the fall, and often that can be the case. It's happened to all of us. It's also true that we all have had many proud moments that always make us feel good when we think about them. Three of those moments for me involved sports.

I was deeply involved with sports in my high school years. They played a major part of keeping me in school and graduating. I played all that I could. It was a sad day when it was all over but a happy day to be approaching graduation. Part of the passage at the end of the year was a sports banquet held in the large Methodist Church. This was for all the high school athletes. Some individual awards were handed out that night. Much to my surprise, when the Methodist Men's Good Sportsmanship Award was given, my name was called. I was shocked. I didn't even know such an award existed but sure enough my name was added to a large trophy that stayed at the church. I have a picture with it being presented to me that I still treasure. That was a proud moment.

Twenty five years later I found myself encouraging my oldest son to play football in high school. He is a big but very gentle guy who until then preferred to play it as a loner. A vision problem made any attempt at childhood baseball or basketball fruitless and therefore he had no interest in ball. After much persuasion, he finally relented to go out his freshmen year for football. I think he knew that he needed exposure to team play to get him out of his shell, but I did promise him that if he would do this one thing, I would never pressure him to play sports again.

The first weeks weren't easy for him and I could tell it wasn't his favorite thing to do. After dinner we would get out in the side yard and practice some of the lineman's stances. One day I was in my offensive lineman's stance and he in his defensive mode. The next thing I knew he was picking me up off the ground. Kindergarten was out. I don't know how much that influenced his love of the game, but he didn't need any more help from me, other than encouragement.

It turns out that he played four years for the Herrin Tigers, earning two varsity letters. At the end of his senior year an all high school sports banquet was held to celebrate the teams and hand out some individual awards. One of the awards made that night was the Christians' Athlete Award to my son. The closest thing they had to a good sportsmanship award. I was so proud of him. You can imagine how I felt when he made an acceptance speech and attributed his love for the game to his dad and gave me much more credit than I deserved. He came out of his shell playing football and never went back in.

My second son also played football for three years but finally had to drop out because of curvature of the spine. He was devastated. I never had to persuade him. He loved all forms of sports and played them from the time they would let him on the field of play. He was able to continue track and the very next year after his brother had won the award, he himself was given the Christian Athlete Award at the sports banquet. I'm sure that brought a few tears that night. Of all the awards at the high school level that are given out, my sons had gotten the best, and maybe I came in a close second place. I wonder if they are still allowed to give that one back in my home town. Political correctness you know.

I also have a daughter. If she had been physically able to compete in high school sports, I dare say there would have been another such award won by a Swinford. My wife and I have always thought she was the most aggressive and hardest worker of the lot, but of course she has had to be. We're so proud of her accomplishments in life and the way she goes about living her life as independently as possible. There is no doubt that if awards were given out in our family, she would get the Christian Award. But we'll leave that award to be given by our Father in heaven, much later we hope. Meantime, we're still very proud of all our children.

THE DAYS OF YOUR LIFE MARILYN

For a time you were the rosy babe in arms to be nuzzled and put on display. About the time you were three years old another baby came along with whom you were to share your life and attention. It was a happy childhood and you were cherished and were a source of great pride to your parents. Another four years brought along a red headed boy whose energy and activities made a significant change to the quiet and serenity of your home life. Now as the big sis you were looked up to and were also responsible for so much more and was increasingly helpful to your mother in many ways. Life was very good, and as you entered your adolescent years you were blessed and had much of the very best of everything, including doting and loving parents.

Awkward teens brought on new challenges but also new friends. There were high spots and low spots as your vision created challenges that would last a lifetime. You made the very best of it and proceeded with life looking forward to college and adulthood. You developed lasting friendships and along the way you met a guy. There would be other guys as the years went by, but one in particular had caught your eye.

You went away from home for the first time for college life and it was a drastic change carrying with it new experiences. You enjoyed the activities, the new friendships, and life on campus as you matured and your horizons expanded. While you stayed in touch with your guy by mail in faraway places, your daily schedules brought you many hours of carefree happiness. The day came though when your priorities said it was time to join with your special guy in starting down a path that would lead to the future and your own family.

Big decisions were made. You wore his ring and you adjusted to the changes. With your joint efforts you overcame many challenges and the two of you started down the path to your life long dreams of a home, a family, a happy life. And now, seventy-eight years after your birth you can look back as a wife, a mother, and a grandmother. I think you fully realize that the joys far exceed the trials and you feel blessed and thankful. Thankful for parents that first loved you, thankful for the opportunities you have had, and thankful that you have a loving family that you can call your own and have influenced all the days of their lives. Be happy with the knowledge that you have helped shape the lives for your family and the families to come that they may have. You are and always will be considered the sweetest most loving person that they may have ever known or ever will know. God has blessed you, and each of them, including your husband of these past fifty-seven years.

SURPRISE BIRTHDAY PARTIES

My wife did a wonderful job of making birthdays special for our children growing up. I'm sure they have many fond memories of food, cake, games, and presents. She knew how to do it because she had a loving mother who did the same for her. On the other hand, being the youngest of eight of a tenant farmer/construction worker I have no memories of parties and presents the first six years of my life. Oh yes, I'm sure Mom probably made my favorite meal and Dad may have even sang to me but honestly I don't recall that ever happening in my life. Not because they didn't love me, but that was the way it was for families scrambling to survive for many years. I'm sure my siblings would say the same.

That is one reason why after many years of marriage I decided my wife needed a special birthday on her sixty-fifth birthday anniversary. So, with the help of my children and the aid of some neighbors we put together a surprise party at the local community center with seventy five guests, including family from out of town. This was a gamble we were taking on a January night in Southern Illinois.

Much preparation was done with special posters and pictures, special music and a program was put together for this special dinner party. We knew that we would need a tremendous amount of luck to pull this off without her finding out about it. Other secrets about pets and such never worked out. The fact is, we did it. We swept her off her feet and the evening was a complete success.

I shouldn't have been surprised though. That wasn't the first surprise party I ever threw. The other was over fifty years earlier when I was in first grade. During that year I was invited to two birthday parties for classmates and I thought they were pretty neat. Two of my older sister advised me that this normally meant buying gifts which surprised me, and somehow I did take something. At the parties we played games and had a lot of fun. So much so that I decided to throw a surprise party myself.

On my birthday I went to school and invited some of my classmates over after school for a party. It was on quick notice but some said they could come. I hurried home from school to beat the others there and told my Mom that I was having a party, much to her surprise. Then the kids started showing up and she and two of my sisters rose to the task. They got out some apples, popped popcorn and made up a couple of games to play. I remember us having a good time. I choose not to remember what my mother and sisters said after it was all over. I had thrown my first surprise birthday party.

REAL HEROES

You can make a man out of a kid, but you can never take the kid out of the man. I don't think that's a Confucius saying, but none the less it's true, if you're a real man. If you were fortunate to have been around in the forties and early fifties, you no doubt had many the same heroes as I have. They were real men with real horses, not some robots, or aliens, or supermen and spiders. They had two legs, two eyes, and normally two six shooters. They walked and talked like real men. For nine cents (if you went before 4 p.m.) you could see those guys at the local theatre each week. Hollywood may have called them 'B' Movies, but they surpassed any 'A' Movie they ever made back then, and besides you got weekly serials and cartoons.

Most of you have heard of the more famous ones like Roy and Gene, the singing cowboys. Roy Rogers on his Palomino Horse Trigger hunted down many a bad man and rustler. There was no mistaking him when things got tough. He was the one with the white hat. That could normally be said about all the good guys with a few exceptions. Then there were some specialist like men with whips. Zoro came later but Whip Wilson and Lash Larue paved the way. There even had a few sidekicks that deserved super stardom like Froggy Milhouse who later went by his real name of Smiley Burnett, and old California, the side kick of Bill Boyd also known as Hopalong Cassidy and his famous horse Topper.

Gene Autry didn't look that tough to me. If fact he was always a little soft around the middle, but he and Champion got the job done and he was really likeable. Tom Mix and his horse Tony was the hero of the generation ahead of me. My Dad would talk glowingly about him. Then there were some of the lesser known ones like Rex Allen, Tex Ritter, Johnny Mack Brown, The Durango Kid and others that just don't come to mind right now. That happens. The Lone Ranger and Tonto came along a little later with their steeds Silver and Paint. And lest I forget, the side kick of more than one was Gabby Hayes. George 'Gabby' Hayes was in the movies much earlier than most of the heroes. He could be seen playing a smooth shaven banker in a black suit in the middle thirties, instead of the fully bearded broken down winey sidekick of Roy, or Gene, or others.

Not all were real heroes, but they stood for honesty and goodness, and the good old American way. Youngsters, you don't know what you missed.

KIMPO AIR FIELD, KOREA

It had been a long day sitting in the terminal waiting for the C-140 Cargo plane to arrive from Pusan on its way to Tokyo. The chance for an R&R in Tokyo didn't come around too often and time was a wasting. I had already read every English magazine in the rack and was hunting for something to do when I saw this thing that resembled a whale coming in for a landing. I picked up my bag and got ready to go to the gate when one of the security guards told me to rest awhile.

It would take some time before this plane would be airborne again. I just threw up my hands.

I stood there for a while and saw the nose of the aircraft open and slowly ramps were lowered to the ground. After a while two jeeps came off the plane. After that the ramps were adjusted and approximately twenty G.I.s came down the ramps. In the meantime I saw what appeared to be the pilots headed for the chow hall and so I knew it was going to take a while.

I asked one of the guards to alert me when the plane started loading again, and then I must have dozed off. When I awoke I saw what seemed to be a company of soldiers with weapons and a tank out near the nose of the plane. The soldiers loaded in first and then the ramps were changed and some heavy equipment was loaded. I started rushing around and trying to find out when I was to get aboard. Things seemed to be almost frantic as everyone was rushing around. Finally I found a clerk and tried to get an explanation. He asked if I was the guy waiting for an R&R ride and I told him I was. He took me in to see his Captain.

I reported in and saluted the Captain and explained my concern about missing the plane. I'd been waiting over six hours. The Captain just stared at me and said, "you've been preempted. Dismissed." I left and sat down again not knowing what I was to do. It was late in the evening so I asked the clerk to call my company for me, which he did. I told the Officer of the Day my predicament. The officer said he'd get back to me. The plane was now taking off without me and I had nowhere to bed down and the Air Force didn't care. They had other things on their minds and they weren't sharing it with me.

That's where I was two hours later when a jeep pulled up outside and one of the sergeants from my company came in. He said get your bag private, we going back to the company. Right then I knew my chances of going on R&R in Japan was slim and none. He didn't have much to say on the return trip but told me to report to the company office before turning in. I walked in and recognized Lieutenant May sitting behind the desk reading. He told me to sit down. He went on to tell me what had happened was the 8th. Army was put on alert because of trouble brewing at the Suez Canal. Often when trouble started one place, it cropped up at others like the 38th. Parallel where the North Koreans faced off against the United Nations allies. All R&R's were cancelled.

I woke up a little late the following morning to a buzz going around the Quonset. I couldn't get the story at first, but then it started to make sense. A U.S. C-140 Cargo ship flying out of Kimpo Air Base the night before had crashed in the Haun River. The attempt to recover any survivors from a company of men was underway but it was feared that the bodies were being swept out to sea. With that news I went completely limp.

When I look back over this story I think of many things, but first and foremost, this story is pure fiction. Other than the animal speaking tails, this is the only made up story in this book.

EXCLAMATIONS!

Happiness, sadness, hurts, surprises, and other things bring on exclamations. There are hundreds of ways of expressing one's self in given circumstances. They start very young in life from the babies crying and end in the last gasp of the dying. Do you have a favorite? Do you habitually let one word or phrase fly into the air whether any one is listening or not? It may not even be a word but a sound that expresses your sudden impulse. Let's concentrate for this discussion on that expression that may be used when hurt, and all have been hurt and experienced pain.

We'll pass over the baby stage as that is not within our grasp of memory. Let's start with the kindergarten toe stub when you are shoeless. I can hear the 'Cry', the 'ouch', mama, and other sounds where the young one does not have an extensive vocabulary. Move on to the ten year old in the school yard who is running and falls on the concrete, not only tearing his pants but skinning his knee. What is he saying? In my day it might have been darn it, or others further south may have said dang it. Ouch would still have been appropriate and more screeching sounds may have been emitted. All sounds of distress.

By the time you have finished your first year of high school, your vocabulary has been immensely expanded, for the better or worse, and so has the exclamations for many. Added to the vocabulary already used in the younger years is profanity. Profanity is taking the Lords name in vain. This spreads widely among the youth and some will never do the Lord's name, but they may learn short cuts such as 'dam it'. That in their mind may be okay. Others turn to vulgarity and it often is used more in public that when they are alone. Alone they may be shaking a fist and moaning and groaning, but in public they may be letting everyone know by their loud pronouncements.

As adults, the extremes have been reached and maturity generally brings a moderation of exclamations. Oh, gosh, phew, may be more prevalent than some of the harsher language of the late teens. Part of this is that some people would prefer not to pass on inappropriate language on to their own children. They have gained some wisdom by this time and no longer are trying to impress anyone with such outrageous language, but some carry on thinking they have no reason to change their life style or language. For these people, the use of bad language normally starts for their young in the household at an earlier age.

As mature adults, we have heard it all. For some, offensive language often marks the character of the person and whether we choose to be around them or not. The nature of society has changed and what was once unacceptable is now getting to be the norm, but our standards are set and some of us will never change. The problem is that our children and grandchildren are exposed now at earlier ages and our control is minimal. You can ban the T.V., but you can't ban the T.V. used by the second grade classmate. You can Charter schools or home school, but you can't influence the neighbor's kids down the block who is exposed daily at home.

Vulgarity and Profanity are just words. Somewhere along the line man determined they were not wanted in our society. This is not unlike Prohibition. It only puts the bad guys in charge. Maybe if they lost their shock value, people would cease to use them to attract attention. This is difficult for Christians I know, but I also know that in my generation I had to ask my Sunday School teacher what a Virgin was. People just didn't use that word. How about fornification or other words that have become more of a norm? True, they were used in the Bible, but not talked about in polite society. Man has created many new words that are not in the Bible. Take the stinger out of the bee and he will sting no more. No one is going to make it unlawful to use what is considered foul language, so maybe we should just learn to ignore it and see how long it lasts.

I feel so blessed that I have an extended family that has not gone overboard on the use of Profanity or Vulgar language. Yes, I've heard Profanity and may have even used some in my life, but I'm not sure of that. I've never used Vulgarity as an exclamation. I may have used the words in discussion. My mother and father now have over one hundred direct descendants, and I don't know all of them, but my bet is that most do pretty well. I hope that the love and faith of Jesus Christ sown in most of the parents in that number still resonates in the off-springs. This brings to mind the exclamation that my own mother used in times of surprise or distress. I can still hear it after almost sixty-five years since she left this earth. "Bless My Soul".….

WILL YOU BE REMEMBERED?

To be remembered by someone who is not family, work acquaintance or friend, will you make the grade? Will the kid down the block remember you? I think that it's nice that we can remember people who may not have had much in life or a lot of family. The fact that we can still remember them is a tribute.

In my age span of seven to eleven I lived on a block called O'Kalla Street. In just writing that, I wished I had an answer for why a street was called by that name. Anyway, it just consisted of two very long blocks. On my block I remember most all my neighbors, but to my point I remember some that had no kids and weren't openly social. They were just ordinary people.

I know why I remember Brock Peters. First of all he had fiery red hair and we called him Red. He could be the most popular guy with all of us at certain times. In mid-summer when it was hot and dusty, and when water just wouldn't do the trick, there were days that Red would come home for lunch or something in the ice truck that he drove for the local elevator. It took a lot of begging but eventually he would casually chip off a piece of ice or two and then the battle was on. Blocks of ice came in fifty and twenty-five pound sizes and I wonder how many household got their full pieces with all the kids around begging.

At the far end of the block was Mr. Richey. With his handlebar mustache and rheumatism, he seemed to be a hundred years old. But now I realize he could have been seventy-five. To make a little extra money Mr. Richey would hire us boys to go dig sassafras roots for him. He knew where to find them and would explain to us on how to get there and what to look for. He even supplied us with a spade to dig them up. We'd carry our find back to him and he would cut them into uniform size and bind them with string. We would get so much a bundle. It wasn't my favorite tea, but I'd like to have a cup just to refresh my memory.

Then, just across the street and down a house were Elmer and Granny Ketner. Don't let the name fool you. They were brothers with Granny the older. Granny was grumpy and one we didn't hang around too much unless we wanted some of his rhubarb. He had an old horse out in the shed beside the house and among other things he would plow gardens for people.

My favorite though was Elmer. Poor old sick Elmer. Once in a while he'd make it out to the front porch swing, but most days he'd spend in his house making doilies to sell. He had different sizes and shapes of framed boards with nail heads sticking out of them, and he could really make a doily fast. He took the time to teach me how to do it, but I couldn't get the hang of it. He couldn't work to long at a time though, he would get coughing spells and would have to stop and cough and spit in one nasty old bucket. You see, Elmer had Tuberculosis. One day when I came home from school my folks or my brothers told me that Elmer had died. The story was that he had sent his nephew, a boy about our age, down to the store where he brought home enough rubbing alcohol for Elmer to consume and die. He was the first person I ever saw laid out in a casket. Rest in peace old friends. You've been remembered.

THE SWEETEST PERSON I HAVE EVER KNOWN

*(Written in memory of his grandmother
by John David Swinford,*

Grandson of Joanne and Owen Swinford)

A beautiful smile,

a warm hug, and a caring hello

Were all treasured gifts from

The sweetest person that I have ever known

"Is there anything you need"

she would say

"Is there something I can do"

These were questions

that came from her heart from

the love that she felt for you

No one could make

you feel as special or make

you feel more at home.

Going to her house was always a privilege, spending time

with the sweetest person I have ever known

To us she was many things:

a grandmother, a sister, a mother, and a wife

But she was also a saint and an angel from God

given so she could touch our lives

from her lips a bad word was never spoken

In her presence you could never feel alone

She was the epitome of kindness,

a person to admire and look up to

The sweetest person I have ever known

God we know you had to take her

Tears fill our eyes as it pains our hearts to see her go

God please wrap your arms around her and

smile into the eyes of Joanne

The sweetest person we have ever known.

IF YOU'RE NOT CONFUSED NOW, YOU SOON WILL BE

As a kid we use to laugh at the old country song, 'I'm my own grandpa'. Have you heard it? Look it up. You can't help but try and figure it all out.

The Swinford confusion may have started a long time ago. My Great Uncle George was the senior of three brothers that were in the Union Army during the Civil War. He was wounded in a battle somewhere along the line but came home to live a long healthy life, except he never had any natural born children. We can only surmise that the injury may have had something to do with that. He married a Rachel Digby and it ended up that they raised what we think was Rachel's niece, Rachel Elizabeth Digby. It is unknown whether the couple ever adopted Rachel or not, but it's possible. They also raised a Frank Whiteside and he became a Swinford, having eleven children and substantially expanding the family name and he was adopted, but that's another story.

So far so good, but now comes along Matthew Simpson Swinford, my Paternal Grandfather. Matthew, born in 1849, was the youngest brother of George. Matthew was still just a kid when George went off to fight for the union. But kids grow up and this one married one Rachel Elizabeth Digby, who might have legally been Swinford, but we'll never know. Things were not that well documented in the 1870s'. I've never seen a copy of the marriage license of my grandparents. Anyway, someone blessed the marriage and it lasted almost sixty years and begot eleven children, nine of whom grew to maturity. That had to be a real marriage.

The last of their bunch, born in 1903, was my father Adren, and as any good Swinford would he had eight children. No confusion about that. I can look back with pride and be very proud that my grandfather Matthew was the son of Elisha Simpson Swinford born in 1803 and that the first three generations of this clan lived for a total of 177 years, and I currently represent the fourth generation and currently am in the 213th year of our reign. But, this is where the water gets a little muddy.

Rachel Elizabeth Digby Swinford Swinford, (note the possible repeat), is my maternal grandmother. But is it all that simple? As George's daughter, isn't she also my grandfather Matthews niece? And if she's my Great Uncle George's daughter, isn't she also my father Adren's cousin, which would make her my first cousin once removed? I'm getting confused already so let's try again.

If Rachel Elizabeth is Uncle George's daughter, and Uncle George's daughter is my maternal grandmother, doesn't that make my Great Uncle George my maternal great grandfather and his wife Rachel my maternal great grandmother? That's so good. I had never traced them before, unlike the Swinford side that goes back to 1760. But wait, if my Great Uncle Geoge is my Great Grandfather, doesn't that make my paternal grandfather Matthew my Great Great Uncle as his younger brother? I'm losing it again.

Whoa! I've got to stop here. I'm already so confused that I may end up illegitimate or non-existent. If the family members are not confused by this time, let them figure it out for themselves. Maybe if you get it all charted you can send me a copy.

ODE TO ANOTHER DAY

I open my eyes and it's still dark, but I feel rested and awake and I know it's around five. My legs are slow to move and the pain in my back is still there, but I'm happy to be alive. I splash my face with water to clear my eyes and take a sip from the faucet, because I have things to do.

Two special friends await me down the hall in the pantry; they are more than ready to start their day. They brush my legs when I open the door to let me know they've been waiting too long. I open the garage door and my dog rushes out; he's been so anxious and is glad there is no rain.

My cat leaps upon the counter near to where we store his food, eager and ready for his next meal. We keep a good variety of wet food for him, sometimes fish, sometimes poultry, all good quality, no imitation but real. We can do this, we can make a little fuss because our lives have been blessed and our animals are important to us.

After his breakfast Sonny Boy is eager also to go out and run in the yard. By this time Ben Has finished his run and is waiting to eat and settle down and waits for a kind word. We are fortunate to have such fine pets, one purchased and one arriving as a stray, and it never fails that they brighten our lives and add something special to each day.

That is generally how my day starts, in my home shared with my wife of fifty-five years. She chooses to sleep until seven and get her well-deserved rest to help repair the wear and tear. Her faithful companions, a husband, her dog and a Siamese cat are here to protect her while she rests, and when she arises at seven she begins looking after us, a job at which she is the best.

AND TIME JUST SLIPS AWAY

There was the time when they played barefoot in the dust wearing bib overalls and calico dresses not bought in any store. There were days when the kitchen table had more hungry mouths than food and some had to leave wanting more.

Many summer days passed in the yard and pastures where teams of kids competed for fun and sometimes the fun turned to anger, but at the end of the day they made truces and peace was restored as the family around the oil lamp did linger.

You got to know one another, be it sister or brother, when you sleep three and sometimes four in a bed. And sometimes it took a little negotiation, which the younger ones couldn't win, to determine who would sleep foot to foot or head to head.

Yes, there was always competition and sometimes they didn't like each other very much under what could be difficult conditions. But, as they matured, without really understanding why or how, the bonds that bound them together were strengthened by many stitches.

Love was never a word they heard daily, it wasn't really something they said and in fact was rarely mentioned. They might love the old horse Star, or Momma's fried chicken or the family dog but never said it out loud under any condition.

As the years passed by, the family grew apart and separate paths were taken by all as other priorities tended to dominate. Building lives wasn't always easy, in fact at times it was very hard, and being absent one from another did a gap in the relationship create.

But, despite the changes, one thing was never forgotten as the years took there toll and their parents were lost. That was the instilled importance of what that family meant to each one of them in their hearts and to the parents they loved the most.

Yes, for them, where each one began and where they would arrive was influenced from the very start. It began with a mother who held a family together with faith and intelligence; she was the glue, and a father with a big heart.

Now the time is slowly slipping away and some of those loved ones are now gone to a better place but the memories still linger on. It will remain like the glow of a full moon on a snowy hill and the lovely words and melody of a song.

And as long as that song lingers on in even one of their hearts, and for as long as each day brings the sun, the family that existed in those times many years ago will live again in the memory of when children played, fought, forgave, and had fun.

THEN THERE WERE THREE

The twilight is coming in our lives, and now there are three. Three remaining to carry the many family memories of our youth. Three who walked many of the same roads and faced the same struggles confronted by what was once this family unit of ten. Why only yesterday after our dad had passed, we were still eight strong. But now we are three. In less than five years we've lost five siblings and one dear sister-in-law. That means that for over seventy years we had survived as the children of this union. Five brothers and three sisters truly blessed for these many years is more than any of us expected or had any idea would be accomplished after losing our mother at age fifty-two. Dad made it to eighty and never realized the fear he mentioned many times of having to bury one of his children. We continued on for over twenty-six years before the inevitable started happening in 2009. First it was sister Eula. The second born in the family had just passed her 85th. anniversary of her birth. Just a month later to the day though sister Hazel was to follow, much too soon. She was just over 83. Joanne, Owen's wife had left us earlier that same year 2009, so that was a most painful year. Three gone so quickly. The year 2010 saw Owen decline and follow his wife of sixty-three years. We're thinking he was happy to be re-joining her. He had been born Christmas 1922, so was over 87 years old. After losing these four in the span of one year, we began to fully realize the sunset was approaching for all of us. Part of our blessing had now passed, but part remained.

We did receive a small reprieve then for a period of eighteen months, but then it was Edna's turn. Just After her 84th. Birthday in November 2012 she left this world for a better one after a prolonged illness. And now there were four. One-half had gone on to meet their maker and four remained for what fate had in store for them.

For some there were on-going health struggles, but still there was a quality of life for each, with each other and with the individual families. If anything, perhaps as the numbers were dwindling, we could feel the loss more each time and drew closer together in spirit, if not physically. The remaining four were born from July of 1930 to January of 1937, a span of six and one-half years. All four of us being boys, we shared the same bedroom and sometimes the same bed. We collected fireflies and put them in a canning jar with a lid so that we'd have a night light, at least for a little while. Too distant in age in some cases to be buddies, but always brothers. Who else on a lonely patch of parched earth would you share the smoking of some dried up corn silk with, forcing the younger ones to puff too so that they couldn't tell mom. Fat chance, she knew. Boys will be boys and we were Adren's sons. Anything we did, he had already done it years before. He would have to apply the belt at times, because that's what fathers do. His father before him did the same. It did tend to keep things in better control when applied wisely.

Many a mile we traveled together as boys and men, and as different as we may be in many ways, we're alike in more. Common values, love of family, good food and music are just a few things we share. Would our mother have been proud of our adult lives? We hope so. Was our dad proud of us as men? We know so.

2012 and 2013 brought on trials for us and we coped the best we could, but when the hill got steeper, the sunset crept closer until brother Dale said enough. He had nothing else to prove, and while he didn't want to leave his beloved wife Barb and lovely family, the burdens were just stacked too high to continue, and he said goodbye. At Eighty-three and a half years, he joined what is now the majority of siblings in heaven. They are now together once again and probably sweetest of all he is seeing his dear mother once again, standing right there beside his father. What a reunion day, February 6, 2014. Now there are three!

FATHER AN AMERICAN CLASSIC

(A son remembers his dad in an article published in the Southern Illinoisan Newspaper, June 27, 1984 First Father's Day after his father's death on November 10, 1983. Newspaper Circulation in excess of Sixty thousand)

It seems like all my heroes are all gone. Gone are Audie Murphy, John Wayne and Adren Swinford. Men who were bigger than life to me, not just as a boy but also as a man. Audie died too young, but John and Adren had relatively long lives ending as old age and disease caught up with them. Of course the one I knew best was Adren, or "Buck" as some of his sisters used to call him, my father.

Dad left us in November of 1983 rather suddenly and when we least expected it, but the way he would have wanted to go. After a routine day of making rounds dad died while playing cards with his friends. One sister out of 11 children survived dad as he was the youngest of 11 children. But to his family he never was nor ever will be the least. Dad didn't leave his wife, his eight children, his three stepchildren, nor his nearly 60 grandchildren any worldly goods. But to us who knew and loved him he left a legacy of pride, a cohesive family unit and memories that will be with us always.

Being the youngest of dad's eight children I didn't get to share as many years with him as my older brothers and sisters did. I've always wished I could have shared those years when dad and mom were young, those hard years when sometimes the gravy was made with water instead of milk, and those years when every two years brought on another Swinford.

Dad's life began on June 16, 1903, in Coles County Illinois not too far from where Abraham Lincoln's father settled when they came to Illinois. Two of dad's sisters didn't live to maturity, but he was the biggest of the lot, growing to 6 feet of sinewy muscle – hence the nickname "Buck". Two of his older brothers served in France during World War I, but dad was too young for that war and probably just as well, he didn't have the instincts to be a warrior, he was definitely a man of peace.

Dad's parents were quite old at 55 and 45 when he was born, but fortunately they lived to ripe old ages and dad was in his upper 20's when he lost his mother. About this time he brought his own young but growing family back to the 80 acres of his family farm to help with family obligations and try to provide for his own brood.

With the Great Depression hard upon the nation this was not to be, and in 1936 the family lost the farm and dad was forced to become a tenant farmer to keep body and soul together. The first such farm was in a rural school district south of Oakland, Ill., called Canaan. The land of milk and honey in biblical times was not so kind in the Great Depression, but one momentous occasion did occur there in 1937. The last of his eight children, but not the least, was born.

Owen, the oldest son, went off to Mr. Roosevelt's Civilian Conservation Corps, and the money that he earned helped to keep the family fed and clothed in those tough years prior to World War II. Dad had to forsake farming and went to carpentry – and with the war industry, life became a little easier for the Swinfords. Dad saw two son-in-laws and one son off to war and one of his daughter's husbands never returned.

He nursed and looked after his own wife but lost her when she was at the young age of 52. That loss after 31 years of marriage was the toughest test that dad ever withstood and there were years when we felt the family cohesiveness might not survive. But finally priorities were set right and the family, by now with many offspring, was alive and well. The grandkids got to know a tender hearted and loving grandfather. Dad reached out and helped those in need regardless who they were, and he was the backbone of his own brothers and sisters as he visited, looked after, and buried all of his own brothers and sisters except one.

When I review the days of dad's life, I see drudgery, back-killing workdays on endless days to feed and raise eight kids. I see unpainted clapboard houses, too hot in the summer and too drafty in the winter to be healthy. I see dad working when he should have been in bed being doctored, and I sensed sorrow that he couldn't provide all that he would have liked to for his wife and kids. But also I could see pride, immense pride, in every son and daughter.

I remember a man with weaknesses, but that is unimportant; because of his family he was a man of love. Yes, he may have had his favorites but he loved us all the same. It was just that he had more memories with some than others – and memory, what a memory he had. Songs that were only sung once in a lifetime fell on our ears never to be heard again. His stories were classics, falling on ears to ignorant to capture them for posterity. And laughter, no man loved to let it out anymore than did our father, who spent more days of his life with a laugh than with a tear. But tears would come too to those light blue eyes that were young to the very end. Tears of joy or sadness, tears over hurt feelings or a small pet, or just tears when memories flooded his potent memory time and time again. They were all dad.

Our dad was a simple man and a loving man and he has left his legacy to each of us in some form. Our mother was something special too, but unfortunately I didn't get to spend enough years with her.

Yes dad was last, but to his family who remembers him with much love, he was never the least. Thank God for sharing him with us.

THE WHITE HOUSE

Along with the Statute of Liberty, The Capitol, and many memorials to presidents and those who served and died in fighting for our nation, the White House is very familiar to all of us, yet few have ever been there. That's why one of the highlights of my career was the invitation to come to the White House to hear President Reagan speak to a group of State and Local Officials. It was an honor to enter that beautiful home of the people though I never got further than the East Room where the conference was held. For a forty-five year old man, born in Coles County, Illinois on a tenant farm, this was a special time.

The homes of my youth were not white. In fact they were a natural wood color that had been weathered by the sun and many storms. They ended up greyish in color. When we moved to town our homes took on colors and looked much better. When the wife and I went off to college we went grey again as the plywood housing built for veterans returning from the war were painted grey. I don't think anyone anticipated that they would last fifteen years, so little effort was put into building them. They lasted just that long as we were the last occupants of two of them before they were demolished.

Things got better after that and we had some nice three bedroom homes to raise our family in and were very happy. When the empty nest came along we started thinking of other options and ended up living and renting apartments for the next twenty years. We were happy and thought this would be how we'd live out our years. No one seriously considers buying a house then they are almost eighty years old, do they?

Well circumstances happened with the loss of a special pet and a house coming up for sale in the neighborhood. The house had a special appeal for both the wife and me, so from our first thought of a change until we purchased a new home was a total of sixty days. We moved rather quickly so our children wouldn't have time to get us committed. What we purchased was a house sitting on the highest knoll in the neighborhood with white pillars on the front. If you put a twelve foot high rod iron fence around it, you'd swear you were in D.C. Well that may be an exaggeration because our home will always be open for visitors and we promise you that you will not be confined to one room. Only in America could a boy go from a four room tenant farm house to the White House where we will enjoy the years the good Lord has remaining for us.

PAYDAY CANDY BAR

After years of hard work the years were showing on their face and in their hair. When I was about thirteen I started worrying about losing my parents and wondered what I would do. Like any kid I was thinking about myself. It was a frequent dream that I had. The youngest of eight, my mother was almost thirty seven when I was born and the depression years had taken a toll. She was up early every morning getting my dad off to work and then the three of us still at home off to school. She always had a large garden and then canned many quarts of vegetables for the winter. She often wore a scarf up around her head to keep her hair out of the way, and always an apron. The house was always immaculate, and when she sat down it normally was with her Bible or at her piano. I didn't know she had high blood pressure. She never complained about not feeling well. I don't remember her staying in bed sick a day in her life until 1952.

It was about the time that I started high school in 1951 that she seemed to have lost some vitality. Instead of being a strict mother guiding us, she was quieter and more visibly conscious of our well-being. My next oldest brother and myself were the only ones still in the nest at that time. She worried about us getting hurt playing sports and when we ran around at night. By the spring of 1952 she had lost considerable weight, but was still there for us. That summer I had the dirtiest job

I ever had crawling inside of furnaces to clean them out. I would come home covered with black coal dust. My clothes were filthy and I left the bathroom grimy, but she knew I was working hard and she insisted on cleaning up after me. It wasn't long after that when she was hospitalized for the first time in her life. I didn't know what to think. Instead of taking her to the local hospital, she was taken to Terre Haute, Indiana to a larger facility twenty five miles away. No one explained why. I just knew she was sick. I don't think they did much more than run some test on her that time, and she was back home taking care of us.

Soon after school started in the fall dad moved my brother and I out of our bedroom. It was there that he then set up a hospital bed for my mother where she would spend most of her time. It was a lighter room and had windows where she could see out and also into the living room. She was there the day I came home with a picture of a girl and showed it to her. I was sharing my first real girlfriend. She smiled an agreed that she was pretty. Just a few days later she was taken back to Terre Haute again and was kept there for a while.

It was on a weekend that my dad asked if I wanted to go over and keep my mother company for the day. I was intimidated by the size of the hospital and all that was going on there. She had a room all of her own and was hooked up to tubes. The one that bothered me most was the one going up into her tiny nose. I don't know what its purpose was. She would nap and like any kid I would get restless. I remember her wanting me to go and find something to eat about lunch time and I felt guilty leaving her there alone. My dad had to go back home and couldn't stay. I don't remember ever finding a cafeteria but I did find a candy bar and coke machine and had some lunch. That's when I got excited and couldn't wait to get back to see her with what I had found.

Mom was awake when I returned and I surprised her with a Payday candy bar that was in the machine. That was her favorite candy because she loved the peanuts and the stuff that held them together. I knew it would make her happy. She took the bar smiling and opened it up and broke off one or two peanuts and put them in her mouth, and then lay the rest on her bedside table. That was about the time that I began to realize that maybe she wasn't supposed to have that type of thing.

A couple of weeks later my mother died at home early on Thanksgiving Morning. Dad woke my older brother, but he didn't wake me until later. As was a custom in his family, he unplugged the electric clock in the kitchen soon after she died, about 4:30 a.m. My brother, not knowing of the tradition saw the unplugged clock and started it again. My worst fears of losing a parent had come true and it would have a lasting effect on me. I don't know the last words that I said to my mother or her to me, but I do remember getting her a Payday Candy bar, and she smiled.

FOR THE RECORD

My parents had thirty three grandchildren and I have memories of each of them except the two that died at child birth or shortly thereafter. I know some of my nieces and nephew much better than others and consequently the number of memories differ, but all are important to me. I have listed them in chronological order to be a part of this record.

1.	Donna Marie Childress Nickles Keef Launier	11-26-42	
2.	Marva Sue Duzan Campbell	1-09-44	
3.	Cheryl Fern Swinford Mullens Smith	7-25-45	
4.	Ronald Wayne Duzan	6-14-46*	3-18-52
5.	Linda Marie Duzan Smith	6-07-47	
6.	Jerry Lynn Swinford	4-24-48	
7.	Harold Allen Nickles	10-22-48	
8.	Janet Ruth Huston Vice	4-22-49	
9.	Stanley Eugene Duzan	6-18-49	
10.	Gary Dale Swinford	2-11-50	
11.	Ray Lamone Duzan	12-22-51*	
12.	Cheryl Ann Swinford Luts	4-17-52	
13.	Brenda Jane Swinford	5-21-52*	5-29-52
14.	David Wayne Swinford	6-17-53	
15.	Wanda Kay Huston Murphy	10-12-53	
16.	Carol Ann Duzan Coffman	12-23-53	
17.	James Cleo Swinford Jr.	12-24-53*	7-22-03
18.	Edwin A. Huston Jr.	10-05-54	
19.	Erwin Ira Swinford	4-23-55	
20.	Robert Keith Swinford	5-12-55	
21.	Charles E. Huston	7-08-56*	2-11-94
22.	Debra Marie Swinford Bell	2-18-57	
23.	Timothy Duzan	6-13-57*	6-13-57
24.	Martin Adren Swinford	8-15-59	
25.	Evan Franklin Swinford	9-06-59	

26.	Ruby Ellen Huston	2-03-60	
27.	Douglas Michael Swinford	2-13-60	
28.	Michael Aaron Swinford	1-16-62*	7-24-65
29.	Matthew Aaron Swinford	2-13-64	
30.	Brian James Swinford	5-25-65	
31.	William Ray Swinford	8-19-66	
32.	Monica Marie Swinford		
	Reed Swinford 2-01-67		
33.	Beth Ellen Swinford Smith	11-08-69	

* deceased

THE NEXT GENERATION

What memories would be complete without a grandparent telling of his grandchildren. Our son Bill married Kimberly Ann Adams on 19 December 1987. They had been high school sweethearts and decided to make life's journey together. They have added to our family four of the most beautiful grandchildren that the world has ever seen. If photos were permitted in this portrait I would have shown you some.

The first to come along was Phillip Riley on January 21st. 1992. With his beautiful brown hair and eyes, he grew up to be a six foot four man, graduated from college and married at the age of 23 to Katie Shultz whom he had known for years through Church connections. She is a beautiful addition to our family also. He is a journalist but has a lifelong love of sports and played basketball. Both are dyed in the wool

Cardinal fans. He is named for his grandfather Phillip and great-grandfather James Riley Eads.

On August 10, 1998 Samuel Brennan was born. He decided he would be a blond and like his brother at the age of seventeen has sprouted up to over six foot tall and loves basketball. His mother was anxious when it had been six years since Riley was born and afraid that might be the end. She prayed for more family and she got one, just like Samuel's mother in the Bible. Now as a junior in high school he has aspirations to go to college and continue playing basketball.

Ross Adren was born December 8, 2002 in the same hospital as his two brothers. Also a brown haired young man with brown eyes, for a while it looked like he might be the football player in the family, being shorter and heavier. Much to everyone's surprise he has had a growing spurt and is quickly catching up with his brothers in height. He's no longer heavy and a football player prospect. He may have a heavier frame and be a real buck like his great grandfather Swinford whose name he bears, Albert Adren Swinford. He will be one handsome man.

Lastly, we think, and certainly unexpected came a pink bundle. On June 8, 2008 Sophia Grace was born. She joined her mother in confronting a household of boys and men who adore and treasure her. She is more outgoing than the shy brothers ever were and keeps the family busy with her ventures. She's a performer, a dancer, a piano player and a planner. She likes to keep things well organized and plans made for each future event. Her hair tends to be on the auburn side of brown. Her name Sophia is shared with her great grandmother Ruby Sophia.

As you can readily understand, this grandparent thinks the next generation will most certainly surpass our generations in talent and accomplishment. Let's wish them peace and love. As far as the Swinford name being carried forward, this next generation will do well. Adren and Ruby have over sixteen male great grandchildren who will carry on the Swinford name.

ONE LAST MEMORY

Soon after Beth was born I turned my life around and rededicated myself to the Lord. I was soon singing in the choir and reading my Bible and praying often. In about 1974 I was asked to serve as a Deacon in my Church which I accepted and took on added responsibilities. We had a new Pastor and I was trying to be helpful to him in any way I could.

I got a call from him early in 1975 telling me that my boys had signed an inquiry and wanted to be baptized. My first thought was that they were too young, but the Pastor asked that he be able to talk to them and advise me about any question I might have. He and the Youth Minister came out to the house and set down at the kitchen table and talked to Brian and Bill at length. When he left he told me my boys had shown the maturity to know what they wanted to do, and that we should let them make that decision.

April 20th. is a very meaningful date to me. The birthdate of my mother. This was the time they chose to be baptized and I was the one to immerse them in the water. They came forward and made their confession of faith and the tears rolled down my face continually through the whole process. I first baptized Brian and then Bill. That was when they were nine years old and eight years old and they have maintained that dedication and belief all the years of their lives.

A couple of years later I was called to serve as an Elder in the same church and accepted that role of leadership, taking on the additional responsibilities. In 1981 my daughter Beth was at Church Camp when she felt the need to be baptized. She and her mother called me and it was decided that she would wait until she got back home and talk to the Pastor about it. Soon after that in August of 1981 at age twelve she walked forward on her walker and dedicated her life to Christ. It was my privilege once again to do the baptism. The memory of carrying her into the water and immersing her will be with me forever. My wife and I are most fortunate to have had three beautiful children who have made the right choices in the important things in their lives, and we thank God for that.

MEMORIES

"**P**recious Memories" is an old family favorite. We've sang it many times over the years, many times with Mom at the piano. We still sing it. Its last line of verse touches me in a very real way and has during this project. It says, 'In the stillness of the midnight, sacred scenes unfold.' Isn't that when memories are most real? In our quiet self? Not all memories are positive, but all have a reason and have influenced my life in many ways. I thank God for my family and my memories. I hope yours are precious also. As the old hymn says, 'may they ever flood my soul.' I call it a hymn even though there is not one reference to God, Jesus, or Heaven, but there is no doubt in my mind that God would put his stamp of approval on this song. Our memories and love of family do create sacred scenes.

THE END

Printed in the United States
By Bookmasters